MODERN ATHLETICS

MODERN ATHLETICS

BY

G. M. BUTLER
President, C.U.A.C., 1920–21

With a Foreword by
P. J. NOEL BAKER

CAMBRIDGE
AT THE UNIVERSITY PRESS
1929

CAMBRIDGE UNIVERSITY PRESS
Cambridge, New York, Melbourne, Madrid, Cape Town,
Singapore, São Paulo, Delhi, Mexico City

Cambridge University Press
The Edinburgh Building, Cambridge CB2 8RU, UK

Published in the United States of America by Cambridge University Press, New York

www.cambridge.org
Information on this title: www.cambridge.org/9781107625624

First published 1929
First paperback edition 2013

A catalogue record for this publication is available from the British Library

ISBN 978-1-107-62562-4 Paperback

*Dedicated
to all those from whom,
in my efforts to teach,
I have learnt so much*

CONTENTS

PLATES

The photographs numbered 11 and 12 on Plate VIII are reproduced by permission of Sport and General Press Agency, and Nos. 33–7 on the same Plate by permission of Mr Max Mills, Southampton.

*available for download from www.cambridge.org/9781107625624

FOREWORD

By Professor P. J. Noel Baker

President, C.U.A.C., 1910–12

The ancient Greeks were the first to create much of what we now think most beautiful and most valuable in the civilization of the West. Among other things, they were the first to create track and field athletics. They thought that track and field athletics were worth a great deal of effort and a great deal of thought; they found in them a source of health and strength for the athlete, a source of pleasure for the spectator, and a source of inspiration for the artist. They believed in the moral discipline of athletic training and they valued both the beauty and the thrill of athletic contests. For these reasons they made of their Olympic Games a national institution of the highest religious, social, and cultural significance.

There are more and more people in Great Britain to-day who think of track and field athletics as the ancient Greeks used to. These people look forward to an ever wider extension of the oldest and the most thrilling of games. They look forward to the time when every city and town throughout the country will have its stadium and when the athletes who use these stadia will be numbered by the hundred thousand. They believe that the social results, both physical and moral, of such a development as this of the game of athletics would be immeasurably good.

Such people will be grateful for this book. They will be grateful to Mr Guy Butler for having written it, and they will be glad that it has been published under the auspices of so eminent a public institution as the Cambridge University Press. Nothing could be more appropriate, for Mr Butler is himself one of the greatest of all Cambridge athletes, he was President of a Cambridge University team which included H. B. Stallard, H. M. Abrahams, and D. G. A. Lowe, and he has a record of athletic service for his University and for the Achilles Club which will rarely be surpassed. Mr Butler has, indeed, every qualification for the task which he has undertaken. He has had the experience of nine wonderful seasons in the first flight of athletic contests; he has competed on three occasions in the Olympic Games; he holds a world's record; he is the possessor of one gold, one silver, and one bronze Olympic medal; on one afternoon at the Paris Games of 1924—and in my belief it was the most brilliant of his many achievements—he twice beat 48 seconds for 400 metres from a standing start. During the whole of his active track career he made a close study of athletics, in respect both of general training and of specialized technique. For some years he had the further experience of applying his theories and of testing their validity as Games Master in an important school. He now offers the results of his study to a wider public in this admirable book.

The book in form is addressed to athletes who are still at school. To them it may have a special value, and there are no Games Masters or schoolboy runners who can afford to be without it. But in fact it will be useful to

athletes of every age and calling. It is admirably con-
structed and admirably concise, and there are few people
who would not profit by its instruction on matters of
general health. The training rules are sound, the advice
to parents and masters are wise and cogent, the exercises
are ingenious and effective, the tables, diagrams, and
illustrations are far more valuable than anything of the
kind which I have seen before.

In conclusion, I can only say that I wish Mr Butler's
book every possible success, and that I hope it may be
the forerunner to an even larger and more comprehensive
work, including those events which for present purposes
he has left out; and I must add, with an emotion born
of an experience as long as Mr Butler's own, how ardently
I wish it had been written twenty years ago.

P. J. NOEL BAKER

PREFACE

My chief object in writing this book is to provide for schoolboys, who are keen to make the most of their training, a means whereby they can get hold of the main principles of modern methods in each event. It is my belief that more can be taught through the eye by means of action photographs, especially excerpts from slow-motion cinematograph films, than by many words; hence the lavish illustrations in this book. I hope also that the chapter on Organization may perhaps be of some assistance to those who have charge of School Sports; if only the lines on which these are run could be brought more up-to-date, it would be an enormous gain for athletics throughout the country. Lastly, although this book does not pretend to deal fully with any of the subjects on which it touches, yet I venture to believe that it will benefit not only the boys for whom it is primarily written, but also the many club athletes who want to improve their performances. Certain events, such as the Pole-Vault, the Discus, the Javelin, and the Hammer, I have omitted because, as yet, I have had no practical experience of them, and also because I doubt the wisdom of their inclusion in the School Sports unless five or six weeks are allowed for them. At the same time I believe them to be excellent events if done properly, and I am in sympathy with Captain F. A. M. Webster's efforts to get as many as possible included in the London Athletic Club's Sports at Stamford Bridge.

I wish to acknowledge most gratefully my indebtedness to Mr John Betts, from whose films I have taken the series of excerpts; to Professor A. V. Hill for some very instructive suggestions on the physiology of training; to Mr G. V. Carey of the Cambridge University Press, who has taken so much trouble in converting the rough diamond of my MS. into a tolerably smooth, if not a polished, stone; also to many friends who in varying ways have been of the greatest assistance to me in the preparation of this book.

G. M. B.

March 1929

CHAPTER I

INTRODUCTORY: MAINLY FOR PARENTS
AND SCHOOLMASTERS

PERHAPS the greatest drawback to the progress of athletics in England lies in the prejudice, deeply embedded in the minds of most men, that success therein depends almost entirely on natural ability. Interest, real lasting enthusiasm, for anything depends to a large extent on its capacity for gripping the mind. Games such as golf, cricket, and tennis hold the interest of their devotees in varying degrees from early youth till second childhood. The reason for the enthusiasm which these games inspire lies, to my mind, in the fact that there is a great deal *in* them. They are, in fact, something more than mere "games"; they are sciences full of possibilities and refinements of skill. About them many books have been written and many more are yet to come, each citing reasons to prove that their own theories and methods are the only ones which can possibly claim the consideration of any reasonable being.

The trouble with athletics is that practically all boys and the majority of men think that a sprinter does a fast Hundred and the high-jumper clears his own height just because Nature cut him out that way. In other words, they think there is very little *in* athletics, though most people do realize that, in order to excel in the longer races, even the man whom Nature has chosen for her own must get himself reasonably fit.

The chief purpose in writing this book is to show that even "ready-made" champions, if there be any, can profit from a study of the technique of their event. In fact, just as any boy with a good eye can become a very reasonable cricketer if he is ready to be taught at the nets,

so can any boy or man who is reasonably well con-
structed become a very decent performer at some branch
of athletics. For, just like cricket, athletics is a science,
and though some branches perhaps are more intricate
than others, yet I have never met any athlete, however
experienced, who thought that he knew all there was to
know about his event.

Personally, however, I have found that the more I
study the subject, the more fascinating it becomes, and
I am certain that thought is not thrown away. Indeed
it would be easy to write a long essay on champions and
others who have improved themselves in a short time,
sometimes out of all knowledge, by tackling their problems in a thoughtful way and persevering with their
experiments in spite of disappointments. My aim, however, is to cut down this introduction as far as possible
so as to get on with the actual subject-matter. Nevertheless I shall pause here to discuss some aspects, which
perhaps may be of interest to parents and schoolmasters,
of the physical, mental and moral effects of athletics on
boys.

PHYSICAL EFFECTS

A great deal has been said and written about over-
strain in athletics. Alarmists make much of the enlarged
heart and early demise of those who do much running
in their youth. As yet, the medical profession as a whole
has not studied the question of overstrain very carefully.
But Professor A. V. Hill has now been carrying out experiments on athletes for several years, both here and in
America; also for those with sufficiently technical minds
there is in *The Lancet* of March 3rd, 1928, a lecture
delivered by Dr Adolphe Abrahams on this very question
—"the physiology of violent exercise in relation to
strain". To summarize expert medical opinion is a
difficult matter, and I hesitate where angels might well

fear to tread; at the same time I must give my opinion, which is backed by considerable experience, both with myself and others, men and boys, during the past twelve years. I think that I err, if anything, on the side of safety, and I do not believe the following conclusions will be contradicted by those who have done most research work on the subject.

PRECAUTIONS. *First*, then, I should say that, if it be at all possible, every boy—or man, for that matter—should be thoroughly overhauled medically before he begins training for any race of a quarter mile and over, especial attention being paid to the time taken by the heart to resume its normal beat after exercise, as shown by the pulse. Here, I admit, there is difficulty for the school doctor dealing with large numbers of boys; nevertheless that reaction of the heart, I am convinced, ought to be taken in every school where this is practicable.

Second. It is a great mistake to run in competition without due preparation. More is said of this in the chapter on Training.

Third. Boys should never be allowed to run more than one exhausting race in an afternoon. After a really hard struggle—this, of course, is a relative term—the heart may not resume its normal beat for several hours, and although this will not harm a certain type, *i.e.* the natural long-distance runner, it is asking for trouble in many cases. Be it noted that this hits both at the custom, still prevailing at some schools, of running off everything on a single day and also at the "Victor Ludorum" system, which has the added demerit of over-emphasizing the individual. I shall deal with this question at more length in the chapter on Organization.

Fourth. Young boys should not be allowed to run long distances. "Long" again is a relative term, and I have made suggestions as to the maximum lengths which seem safe at the various ages (see page 12).

So much for the negative side. On the positive side you have a fine system of physical training, building up stamina and developing not only the legs but almost every muscle of the body, especially the heart and lungs, if the training is correctly carried out.

MENTAL EFFECTS

There is a certain danger for the highly strung boy, who may find that, if he is running in competition, the thoughts of the race tend to fill his mind to the exclusion of his work. Probably it is the exception rather than the rule when this worry persists; nevertheless I myself have been troubled by "nerves" and it may not be amiss to give what I have found to be the best remedies. The conscious side of the worry may be dealt with by a calm consideration of the importance of the race in (*a*) the world's history, (*b*) one's own life. A little thought on these lines, I find, does help to restore a sense of humour and to get things in proportion. But unfortunately the conscious side is not the most insidious trouble. It is the subconscious which is often the greatest enemy to thought-concentration, and this I have found can be dealt with most effectively by auto-suggestion. I have outlined the methods in Appendix B (page 140) for those who care to look therein.

On the other hand, Mind plays a considerable part in athletics; for each branch, especially the field events, presents its own special problem. To attain the style which will produce the best results for your own self needs careful thought. Indeed it would not be exaggerating to say that those who have given the deepest consideration to their problems are the successful athletes, though not necessarily the most physically gifted in the first place. Of course, it is difficult to think things out unless you have previous knowledge. Hence this book, which attempts to give the elements of the modern style in each event, so that, with the printed matter plus the photographs, it may be possible to acquire a sound basis upon which each can build his own theories and thereby solve his own difficulties.

MORAL EFFECTS

It is not impossible for the really successful boy athlete to get his "head turned" by over-much adulation. At the same time there are two things which strongly militate against conceit in athletics: first, enthusiasm to do well for your team, and, second, a real interest in athletics for its own sake as an art and science rolled into one. It is generally the thoughtless and ignorant who think most of themselves and least of the game.

Practically all schools now run their Sports on inter-house lines and in most of them the relay race is coming to the fore. Rivalry between houses is, I think, to be encouraged, as the keener it is, the more it not only tends to lay the emphasis on "team" rather than "self" but also means that boys will become enthusiastic enough to coach and criticize each other. Moreover, directly they try to teach anyone else they themselves begin to learn and want to go into the details of action. Such is my experience, and despite the varying forms of conservatism, I believe that on these lines keenness can be stimulated at any school.

Success in athletics generally demands a great deal of hard work, though it may be possible for a boy at school, but not after, to carry everything before him on his natural ability alone, more especially in a place where there is no real attempt at scientific athletics. Whether the events be cross-country running or high jumping, there is, in their different spheres, the same demand for keenness and persistence in the face of disappointment. It is a comparatively easy matter to produce the extra yard or two necessary to win a race when you are keyed up to it and everyone is watching you, but it is an infinitely harder business to carry through a scheme of training when there is no one to applaud your efforts. But, given the encouragement and a certain amount of knowledge, boys will work really hard with wonderful enthusiasm. And this is where the character-building value comes in.

SUMMARY

Athletics, then, when run on the right lines and tackled intelligently, are a game which will have splendid effects in developing physique and turning out really healthy, strong men. They will provide an interest to occupy boys' minds, once keenness is stimulated. The training also will test and strengthen their moral fibre, especially when it is emphasized that what matters is, not individual performances and the breaking of records, but rather doing their bit, great or small, for house or school.

CHAPTER II

ORGANIZATION

THIS subject demands a whole book if it is to be dealt with adequately; however, I must try to do what I can in a small space. It will be best to split the chapter up into three parts. In the first will be outlined a general scheme for Sports at a Public School, which will doubtless seem ambitious to many people, but is nevertheless possible, as I know from my own experience. The second concerns itself with the possibilities of improving the education of boys in matters athletic, and also with methods of training and coaching before the heats of the Sports begin. The third deals with organization on the ground during competition.

None of the suggestions made here are merely theoretical, as they have all been actually carried out; yet I feel a trifle diffident in making them, realizing, as I do, how various the conditions are at different schools and how conservative the customs. Nevertheless I think it may be worth while putting my experience, such as it is, at the service of others who are doing the same work, but perhaps have not had so much time to think things out or such ideal conditions in which to work as I have had.

A GENERAL SCHEME OF ARRANGEMENT FOR THE SPORTS

One of the first questions that arises is how much of the term is to be allowed for the Sports. The answer, so far as this chapter is concerned, is that, if the scheme herein suggested be carried out, there must be a good month to do it in and, if possible, a week before the heats start, to allow boys to do some training. But here straightway is met the problem which probably concerns the schoolmaster more than anything else connected with the Sports—if all this time is given up to the Sports, what guarantee is there that all the boys will, on the one hand, get exercise, and, on the other, be kept out of mischief each afternoon?

The great difficulty of course is that those who are naturally athletic get through to the finals and have very often more than enough to do, while the rest, if they enter for the heats at all, are speedily eliminated and spend the rest of the term, perhaps, watching the athletes disport themselves, and probably eating too much the while. Now if this were an unavoidable situation, it would be a very serious argument for cutting out athletics from the school's calendar, as it seems to me vital that all the boys should have regular exercise combined so far as possible with amusement. Therefore, before going any further, I want to suggest a scheme whereby the whole school does get its exercise every afternoon—and also a good deal of fun into the bargain.

Later on, a plan will be indicated by which all the boys will do a certain amount of training to get them fit and also will be taught a few of the fundamentals of athletics before the heats actually begin. The scheme which I am trying to describe now is intended to occupy all those who are definitely out of all school heats.

INTER-HOUSE LEAGUE RELAYS

This is a system arranged as follows. The staff-work is done by a master and one responsible boy in each house. Every evening in the term, after the heats have begun, the names of all those who are no longer in for any event in the School Sports are collected by these boys and sent in to the master, under two headings, senior and junior. These names are taken by him and made up into senior and junior relay teams of four each. Heats are then arranged, which should be, as far as possible, inter-house affairs. Each afternoon these heats are run off, if possible on a separate track. For the seniors each stage might perhaps be one of 440 or 220 yards, and for the juniors one of 220 or 110 yards. The teams are made up each evening at random, quite irrespective of the abilities of the runners, and very rarely should a boy find himself in the same four two days in succession. Juniors are under no circumstances allowed to compete in the senior relays and no boy must run more than once in an afternoon.

Points are counted on the same principle as in cross-country races, *i.e.* the first team in each heat gets 1 point, the second 2, and so on. The numbers available from each house will of course fluctuate as more and more are eliminated from the heats of the School Sports, so that the scoring is worked on a system of averages. For example, one house may in an afternoon have three teams running, and these may gain second, third, and fifth places in their respective heats. Its total number of points will be 10, which, being divided by 3, gives an average of 3·3. Another house perhaps has more boys out of school heats and has five teams performing, who together amass 17 points. Their average is then 3·4, *i.e.* a shade worse than the former.

I have now seen this system working with considerable success for several years, but it seems to me essential that it should be taken light-heartedly. If this be so, the boys will enter into the spirit of the thing with zest, and indeed I have often seen a large troop of boys pouring round the track urging the representatives of their own houses to put their best foot foremost. At times there have even been gala days in which fancy dress is allowed, and historical characters, such as Boadicea, have put in an appearance. In fact, the more variety and fun there is in it, the more will boys be occupied during the afternoon. Sack, obstacle, and three- or four-legged relays might be introduced now and again to dispel monotony; and if it will not add too much to the seriousness of the business, small challenge cups could be presented for houses winning the senior and junior relays.

INTER-HOUSE RELAYS

Perhaps of all the methods for encouraging the team, as opposed to the individual, spirit in athletics, relay racing is the best. Let that be my excuse for dealing with it before the individual events of the School Sports. In practically every school now there is one relay event in the Sports, but in many cases it has gone no further than that. The relay system, however, is capable of considerable development. There are, in fact, at least seven relay events which can be run off as an inter-house competition, with a cup for the house getting the largest number of points and a silver-mounted baton for each event. These, excluding possible junior events, are:

Two Miles (four half-miles)
One Mile (four quarter-miles)
Half- or Quarter-Mile (four 220 or 110 yards) $\Big\}$. Teams of four.
480 Yards Hurdles (four 120 yards)
High Jump
Long Jump $\Big\}$. Teams of three.
Putting the Weight

The Two Miles is the longest relay race which is likely to produce interesting competition among boys. When teams of first-class milers are opposed, the race may be extremely thrilling, because the runners are good enough to be evenly matched; but with boys the Four Mile Relay tends too much to become a procession. It is possible that in an inter-school relay meeting, when it is desired to make the competitions as fair as possible for the school which is strong in long-distance runners, a "medley relay" may be introduced, possibly over Three Miles with two mile and two half-mile stages. On the whole, however, both at school and elsewhere, the Medley Relay is a mistake.

Until quite recently there was in the Amateur Championships a Mile Medley Relay, which was split up into stages of two furlongs, a quarter-, and a half-mile. In a race of this kind everything is likely to depend on the half-miler, who, if he runs first, may well establish an overwhelming lead, and can in any case make up far more ground than the quarter or furlong runner can possibly do.

The 480 Yards Hurdle race is run backwards and forwards, if possible over alternate flights of hurdles. No baton is carried, but, to quote from the rule as it stands for the Inter-County Relay Championship, "a warning line is drawn 1 yard behind the 'take-over' line, and each competitor must stand on this, and no part of his body must cross the 'take-over' line until he has been touched on the body (and not on the outstretched arm or hand) by the previous runner".

It is inadvisable to have more than three in each field-event team (hurdles excepted), to avoid making the competition tedious. In order to save time, the first rounds of the two jumps, and possibly of the "shot", in the individual Sports may be utilized to decide the relay competition, the three best performances in each house being taken. Should there be juniors jumping, they may be passed through into the finals of their own class if they have come up to the necessary standard. In the other relay events it is a great mistake to allow juniors into the house relay teams, however efficient they may be. Many promising hurdlers have been permanently spoilt by trying to tackle big hurdles before they are strong enough. Their style goes to pieces; they lose confidence, and probably sprain an ankle into the bargain. In the running events also there is danger, especially for the big youngster with a good turn of speed. He is set a big task in making up a deficit on the leading house and runs himself to a standstill in his effort to do so. I have dealt more fully with the technique of relay racing in Chapter XI and there are rules for the same on p. 148 in Appendix D.

THE SCHOOL INDIVIDUAL SPORTS

The first point to be dealt with is the classes into which the boys should be divided. The following suggestions seem to me to provide about the best working scheme, though perfection is elusive. The school may be split up into three classes:

(1) Senior, in which no one under 16 is allowed to compete.

(2) Under 16 and over 5 ft. 2 in.

(3) Under 16 and under 5 ft. 2 in.

This method of taking height as a standard was used at Osborne with satisfactory results and, although personally I have not seen it working, I believe that it should tend to be more efficacious than the more common age divisions for those under sixteen. Here is also a possible list of events for these three classes.

Senior Events. Mile, Half, Quarter, Furlong, and 100 Yards flat races; 120 Yards Hurdles, 3 ft. 4 in. high with standard 10 yd. intervals; High and Long Jumps, Putting the Shot (12 lb.).

Junior Events. A. Under 16 and over 5 ft. 2 in. Quarter-Mile for over 14 years only, 200 Yards, and 80 Yards flat races; 110 Yards Hurdles, 3 ft. high with 9 yd. intervals; High and Long Jumps, Putting the Shot (8 lb.).

Junior Events. B. Under 16 and under 5 ft. 2 in. 150 Yards and 70 Yards flat races; 105 Yards Hurdles, 2 ft. 10 in. high with $8\frac{1}{2}$ yd. intervals; High and Long Jumps.

It seems wise to limit the junior Quarter-Mile to 15-year-olders, for although quite a number of young boys who are natural middle- and long-distance runners would harm themselves not at all over a quarter-mile, or even over distances up to a mile, there must always be considered the determined person who is not really up to it physically but would rather die than fall out; it does not seem fair to sacrifice him. The results, it is true, may not be immediately apparent and are probably hard to prove medically, yet to my mind there is little doubt that if young boys are overstrained, their physical development seems in some way to be stunted. How many boys, I wonder, have done brilliantly at the ages of 15 and 16 but have failed to realize expectations as they grow older. It is perhaps unwise to be dogmatic about such a subject, in which there is so much research work yet to be done, but it does seem to me that the cause is simply that they did do so brilliantly, and suffered some form of strain thereby.

One of the most striking examples that have come within my experience happened a year or two ago and seems worth a digression to give in detail. I was helping with his training a boy who was a very promising middle-distance runner with a beautiful style. Just before the heats of the School Sports began was the cross-country race. He had not trained for it and had entered for four or five events in the School Sports, but wanted to run in order to get his house an odd point or two. I strongly advised against it and told him that it would probably prejudice his chances for the Public School Sports, if not his whole athletic career in the future. In the end he did run in the Cross-Country and did get his house a few points. He also was extremely successful in the School Sports and finished by winning his event in the Public School Sports in a good time on a windy day. Next October he went up to his University with the highest hopes of getting a "Blue", which indeed he should have done even in a good year. Something, however, had gone wrong; the style and stride were still there, but his running lacked life and he "died away" at the end of a race. In his last year he did get a "Blue", but was perhaps a trifle lucky to do so, for even then he was not showing form very much in advance of his last year at school. I cite this example because I believe that there are many who suffer in the same way, and it does seem that something drastic ought to be done to prevent this possibility.

This brings me to another problem which demands consideration. When up at Cambridge I was a keen advocate for limiting the number of events in which an individual could compete in the Inter-College competition. Although, as far as I can remember, this was not done when I was "up", it has come in subsequently. The question is why should this not be done in all School Sports. It seems to me that such a limitation has at least two first-rate arguments in its favour: (1) it will tend to minimize the chance of overstrain, which is an especial danger for two types of boy, the natural athlete who is generally wanted to do far too much in order to get points, and also the enthusiast who is not much good but is mad keen to do all he can for his house; (2) it makes it impossible for a house (or school) to be a one-man team, *i.e.* it gives the others a chance.

Whether it is possible to arrange the rules for such a limitation in an absolutely equitable way seems to me of quite secondary importance. There is one principle which is surely elementary. Whatever the competition be, international, inter-'Varsity, or merely inter-house, no one responsible has the least right to risk the future health of any member of the team. With boys it is natural enough that such matters should have little weight, but for masters who have charge of the athletics it should be a first consideration.

To return to the practical consideration of the best form of limitation: it would seem to be a problem which each school must decide for itself. Perhaps the fairest plan would be that "no boy may enter for more than two flat races and two field events, making four in all". This would also have the effect of emphasizing the importance of the field events, which I think would be desirable.

I fear, however, that the suggestion will meet with a horrified disapproval from the reactionaries. So well do I know their two pet arguments. One is about "the-good-old-days-when-everyone-went-in-for-every-event-and-they-were-all-run-off-on-the-same-afternoon-and-no-one-was-ever-the-worse-for-it". But I wonder! Anyhow it was a long time ago, or should have been. According to my own experience such a system (or should I say lack of system?) had two effects: (1) the faster a boy could run, the greater was the chance that he would do himself serious harm; (2) it ignored every possibility of showing boys that each event has a skill all its own and that athletics, just as much as cricket or football, is cram-full of potentialities for those who care to try.

The other cry is "away with this American specialization!" But is this logical? Suppose the brawniest member of the school XV were taken out of the scrum and turned on to play wing three-quarter without any previous coaching. The result would be that he would make a very pretty mess of things, and there is little doubt in what quarter criticism would be loudest. Or again suppose that no effort were made to coach anyone in the nets in the summer term, what would be said then? Yet it may be that the technique of the sprinter, hurdler, or high jumper who knows his job is something on a par with that of the three-quarter or batsman who knows his. Why then should not the athletic events be taught at schools just as much as cricket or football? Answer: Because it never used to be done in the old days. If you really get down to the root of the reactionaries' objection to the modern view of athletics, it is that it *is* modern and they instinctively react against anything "new-fangled", as they would call it.

After which somewhat lengthy digression we must consider what are the best rules for the individual entries. It is indeed a vexed question whether they should be (1) compulsory for all, (2) entirely voluntary, (3) restricted to those who have some sort of proficiency. Perhaps a combination of the second and third is best. Probably the captains of athletics in the various houses should on the one hand encourage all those who show any promise at all to put their names down, and on the other restrain those who enter in the hopes of providing a "comic turn". Boys, for example, who enter for the Mile when they can hardly run the distance merely cumber the ground and waste time. The right of refusing an entry should therefore, I think, be vested in the captain of school athletics.

The first round or two should preferably be arranged so that the talent is fairly equally divided among the heats. A small committee of three, consisting of the master in charge with the captain and secretary of school athletics, can best undertake this somewhat onerous task. In order to insure smooth working of the programme I have found it necessary to insist on absolute punctuality. Names of all those running should be read over five minutes before the heats of each race begin, and if anyone is late, whoever he be, he may not compete. How many places should count in each heat is a difficult problem depending much on the conditions. If there be four rounds of heats, at least two should be taken from each in the first two rounds, and three in the semi-final.

Points for the Inter-House Cup. It is suggested that, if possible, six places should count points in the finals of the Senior events. This is restricted by the number that can run together in the final heats and also by the difficulty of judging so many places. I have found by experience, however, that six places *can* be taken so long as the judges know their business and have had some experience in the heats (see pp. 26–7). The first thing in favour of this plan is that it puts a premium on the well-balanced house team, and secondly it encourages more boys to try their best. The following is a workable scale of points, which, however, I have not space to discuss in detail.

	1st	2nd	3rd	4th	5th	6th
Senior Events	12	10	8	6	4	2
Under 16 *A* (over 5 ft. 2 in.)	4	3	2	1	.	.
Under 16 *B* (under 5 ft. 2 in.)	3	2	1	.	.	.

Suggestions for outfit to be provided by the school. A cinder track is of course a tremendous asset. It makes the Sports more or less independent of weather, improves performances, and generally tends to stimulate keenness. Its disadvantage lies in the fact that, if it is badly kept— and it needs a certain amount of attention throughout the year—the surface will become a mere sandy waste, not nearly so good as decent turf. If, however, a cinder track is not available, a level field makes a very good substitute so long as it is above water. The only points where cinder has a great advantage are those where there is very heavy wear and tear, such as the High Jump take-off, the run-up for the Long Jump, and the circle for the Weight. Should it be at all possible to have these laid down with cinders on a good deep foundation, the gain will be very considerable. Throughout this chapter and in the following list I have taken it for granted that there is no track and that the Sports take place on a field.

I. Hurdles are the most expensive item. There should be four to six flights. Fig. 1 shows a hurdle which has now been in use for two seasons and has proved most successful. Briefly, the following are its advantages: (1) It

TOP OF HURDLE

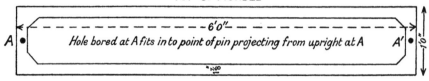

A • — — — — — — — — — — — 6'0" — — — — — — — — — — — • A'

Hole bored at A fits in to point of pin projecting from upright at A

1'0"

1⅛"

FRAME OF HURDLE

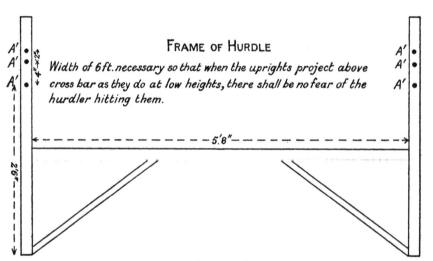

A' •
A' •
A' •

A' •
A' •
A' •

4"×2½"

Width of 6 ft. necessary so that when the uprights project above
cross bar as they do at low heights, there shall be no fear of the
hurdler hitting them.

— — — — — — — — — — 5'8" — — — — — — — —

2'6"

SIDE VIEW OF FRAME

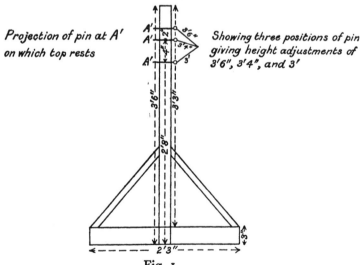

Projection of pin at A'
on which top rests

A'
A'
A'

4"×2½"

3'6"
3'4"
3'

Showing three positions of pin
giving height adjustments of
3'6", 3'4", and 3'

3'6"
3'3"
2'8"

3"

— — — — 2'3" — — — —

Fig. I

has a knock-off top, which is caught as it falls by a cord attached to each upright and can thus be put back quickly and easily. (2) It is adjustable to any height at which holes are bored in the upright. (3) The framework of the hurdle is solidly made and the legs long enough to ensure its standing up in the strongest wind, while the fact that the top falls off so easily almost entirely eliminates breakages, which form such a big item of expense with most other types when used by novices. (4) It is easily and cheaply made.

The disadvantages which I have found in working with this hurdle are (a) that it knocks off only one way, which is inconvenient in relay races unless alternate flights are used; (b) that the pins are inclined to get stuck in the holes in the uprights, though this could probably be put right by greasing them.

If other hurdles are used which have not got knock-off tops, they should be made light enough to "give" very easily when touched. Nothing is more ruinous to good hurdling than alarming obstacles which cause injuries when hit. Doubtless knock-off tops in competition tend to spoil boys, i.e. to make things almost too easy, but I believe that it is a fault in the right direction when they are learning (see also Chapter VII on Hurdling).

II. If at all possible, there should be two High and two Long Jump pits, one of each for practice. It is essential that these should be amply large and well filled with sand. The measurements suggested are: for the High Jump, 15 ft. by 10 ft.; for the Long Jump, 15 ft. by 5 ft. 6 in., with 10 ft. between the take-off board and the edge of the pit.

These figures may seem fantastic to many people; but they are none too big, as I know from bitter experience of broken wrists in the High Jump and sprained ankles in the Long. It must be remembered that the average inexperienced high jumper, who depends on speed in the run-up, clears as much as 14 ft. from take-off to landing; and the long jumper who jumps 19 ft. in length very often falls forward another 4 ft. or 5 ft. with considerable force, while the direction even of some expert long jumpers is bad, so that, unless the pit is amply wide, they may well land with one foot on the edge. If it can be managed, there should be a two-way run-up for both jumps, and the ground must be level. The merit of the approach from either end is that it will not be necessary to jump against the wind, which is a somewhat devastating proceeding, and also the take-off will not get so worn.

For the Long Jump the take-off boards should be of ample dimensions. The maximum, as laid down in the A.A.A. laws, is "not more than 4 ft. long, 8 in. wide and 4 in. deep", and this is an ideal to be aimed at if possible. In order to facilitate accurate measurement, it is absolutely essential that there should be two measurement boards, one on either side of the pit, both marked alike, as in Fig. 2, which also shows the correct method of measuring a jump.

III. There should be a measuring-rod for the High Jump, and the winning height should be taken from the centre of the bar, which sags sometimes as much as 2 inches.

IV. There should be a plentiful supply of wooden pegs, made flat for writing on and amply sharp. These are a necessity for the Long Jump and Shot (see p. 27).

V. A revolver is best for purposes of starting, as a second barrel is sometimes wanted to stop the runners in case of a false start.

VI. Two or three stop-watches should be available. The split-second variety is the best, as it is doubly useful for taking the exact time of the laps without stopping the watch and also for taking second, or even more, places in the longer races.

VII. Two toe-boards for the Shot and two pairs of

High Jump standards, one of each for purposes of practice.

VIII. A good number of batons for relay racing.

IX. A tape-measure should always be handy and is a necessity at the Shot.

X. A black-board is a great asset for putting up the points both in inter-school matches and also in the finals of the Sports.

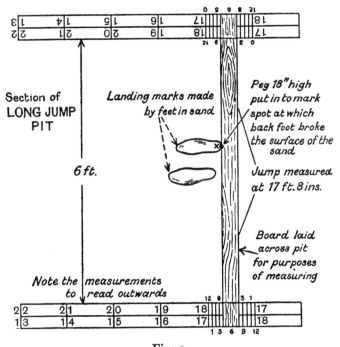

Fig. 2

XI. Though these of course will not be provided by the school, it is of great importance that the boys should be fitted out with good, tight-fitting shoes. A slovenly, loose running-shoe has the same effect upon a runner as a slipping clutch on a car. Shoes for sprinting and jumping especially should fit quite as tight as the white kid gloves which have caused so much suffering to those of us who dance. These shoes stretch very quickly;

indeed, if I remember rightly, once when I was up at Cambridge I spent over an hour struggling into a pair of sprinting-shoes which had to be discarded as too large after twelve months' wear.

In some schools where individuals cannot afford their own shoes a fund has been raised which is gradually providing a central supply for hiring out to boys who want them. This seems an excellent scheme, as shoes are an absolute necessity in practically all the field events, as well as in sprinting. A crouch start in "plimsolls" on slippery grass is merely a farce.

WHAT CAN BE DONE BEFORE THE HEATS BEGIN

LECTURES. The best way of teaching boys about athletics and at the same time stimulating enthusiasm is by means of lectures on half-holiday evenings. Slides are of course a great asset—almost, in fact, a necessity, and the cinema has, I am sure, a big future in this connection. Personally I have started a series of lectures of about half to three-quarters of an hour each, taking "Training Principles" as the first subject, then working through others such as "Middle-Distance Running, Sprinting, High Jump, Long Jump, Hurdling, Putting the Weight".

Some of the history of athletics could be worked in well here, and for this purpose slides of the Olympic Games can be borrowed from the British Olympic Association. This, of course, takes a good deal of time and trouble for masters; but I have made the suggestion in case it may be possible for some enthusiast to take it up, and I have also added a bibliography in Appendix A (p. 139) in case of need.

INDOOR COACHING. Some of the field events are so difficult that in order to master even the principles of their technique it is necessary to do some coaching before the Sports begin. The best place for this is generally the

Gymnasium. Hurdling over one hurdle, which is the only way to teach it successfully, and high jumping, with an ample supply of mattresses on which to fall, are both rich in results. Once a week throughout both winter terms is not too often; only of course the attendance, as in the case of the lectures, must be voluntary. Much more could be said on this subject, but space is limited.

DEMONSTRATIONS. Another very efficacious method of teaching is by means of personal demonstration, and if the master in charge of the Sports is an athlete himself there should be no difficulty in carrying out the following suggestions, which are all explained in detail elsewhere in the book.

(1) "*Limbering up*" (see p. 63): (*a*) Touching toes. (*b*) High kicking. (*c*) Striding with (i) knee-lift, (ii) hip-swing.

(2) *Running:* (*a*) Striding action: its use in practice and competition contrasted and explained. (*b*) Sprinting and its uses. (*c*) "Cornering." (*d*) Judgment of speed. A certain distance should be attempted in a set time and the pistol fired when the time has elapsed.

(3) *Track Tactics:* (*a*) The folly of passing on a corner. Two or three run abreast up to a corner; as they round it each must keep his original speed, so that it may be clearly seen how the outside runners lose ground. (*b*) How to "jump" your man when passing him (see p. 64).

(4) *The "crouch" start,* showing the chief faults (Chapter VI).

(5) *Passing the baton* correctly and also with the usual mistakes (pp. 135–7).

(6) How to get the right run-up for the Long Jump (pp. 119–121).

If possible, experts should be persuaded to come down to the school to demonstrate the various field events such as hurdling, shot putting, high and long jumping.

TRAINING RUNS. Before the heats begin, it is an excellent thing to send out the whole school for training runs over a mile or so. Every athlete beginning training should do some slow "distance" work, *i.e.* at distances longer than his actual event, whether it be the sprints or middle distance. Needless to say, these runs should be taken at a slow pace, as they are intended to tone up the muscles of the heart and the lungs. Many people hold that boys at school are naturally so fit that they do not need this preparation. Personally I am strongly of the opinion that they *do* need it. Being "in training" for football is not the same thing as being fit for a Quarter or Half-Mile, and one or two runs of this type, I believe, are most beneficial (see pp. 136–7).

A good method of working this is by dividing each house up into fast, slow, and perhaps medium packs. A course of about $1\frac{1}{2}$ to 2 miles in length is chosen, and each pack aims to cover the distance in a certain time. Each pack-leader must have a wrist- or stop-watch and must himself take the lead. In order that this scheme may work smoothly a certain amount of staff-work is necessary. The times of the various packs have to be determined by personal experiment and each pack must be started off absolutely punctually with a certain time-interval.

METHODS OF COACHING ON THE FIELD

Coaching, when once the heats have begun, is a difficult business. Except in relation to the more promising performers, one's activities tend to be limited to preventing boys doing too much (see Chapter III on Training, pp. 33–6 also p. 62). Most of the really useful teaching will have been done in the Gymnasium before the heats begin. There are, however, some methods of dealing with large numbers, and I think they are helpful.

Starting practice may be given for a fair number, and

PLATE I

I   2   3   4   5

Voluntary starting practice for all classes of runners with appropriate handicaps. This photograph and others like it were taken so that the form of the boys could be criticized. Reading from left to right here are a few obvious criticisms: No. 1 is too upright and is not using his arms to advantage. Nos. 2 and 4 have allowed their right arms to fly back unflexed and hence out of control so as to slow up their actions. No. 3 is showing good form and in point of fact, although a heavyweight, he was very quick off the mark.

the "crouch" start, if taken very much in moderation, is, I am sure, a splendid exercise for every class of athlete. I had 15–20 lanes marked out in a corner of the field and used to have handicap races over 50 yards for anyone who cared to come along each afternoon before the heats began (see Pl. I).

In order to develop speed, a game of "follow my leader" has great possibilities. A large number of boys may be strung out round the track, each 2 to 4 yards behind the other, with the slowest in front. The master of ceremonies stands in the middle of the ground with his starting revolver, and at the first shot they all start trotting slowly round the track, strictly keeping their intervals. At the second shot each goes "all out" to catch the man in front. After three or four seconds a third shot is fired, when the chase ceases and the order is re-sorted, those who have been caught going one place forward and the catchers one place back.

Pace-judgment is one of the most important things a runner can learn. It should be the aim of every boy to emulate A. G. Hill, the great middle-distance runner, who could tell his time over each lap within $\frac{1}{5}$ second. The following is one of the best ways of teaching it. A set time of, say, 68 seconds is given for the lap of a quarter-mile. Each runner is started with the revolver and runs at uniform speed until another shot is fired when the time has elapsed, so that he can see his error.

It is obviously impossible for the Sports master to supervise all the coaching himself. But when the boys begin to learn a certain amount about their own specialities, they can with great advantage look after the beginners and often become really useful coaches after a little experience is gained, especially if they are keen enough to read about it on their own (see Bibliography, p. 139).

ORGANIZATION DURING COMPETITION

OFFICIALS. A badly run Sports meeting with unnecessary pauses, especially in the sort of weather with
which we are blessed in our English March, is of all
things the most tiresome. The programme on each afternoon, whether of heats or finals, should work strictly to
time, and it is not difficult to bring this about with a
certain amount of forethought. The first need is a goodly
band of officials who are amenable to discipline; hence
they are best recruited from the boys, though the starter
and referee should, I think, both be masters.

Judges. The number of judges will depend on how
many places are to be taken. If, however, it be six in
the finals, as suggested, they will have to know their
business and should have had some experience in the
heats. There are two important things which they must
remember: (1) that they should be well back, some 10
or 20 feet from the tape, in order that their eyes may have
all the runners in perspective; (2) that they should not
follow the struggles of the runners in the last stage of
the race, but keep their eyes riveted on the tape itself.
More faulty decisions have been given from a disregard
of these rules than from anything else. I wonder how
many action photographs of the finish of a school 100
Yards show the judges standing right up against the
finishing-post, while one of them at least is looking at
the runners rather than along the tape.

Time-keepers. The time-keepers also will be somewhere
near the judges, and the above rules apply to both. It
may not be amiss to give a reminder that time is taken
from the flash of the pistol and not from the report. If
it be taken by sound in a 100 Yards race, it will make
the time shorter, *i.e.* faster, by about $\frac{3}{10}$ second, which
is approximately a little over 2 yards.

Stewards. A certain number of stewards will be necessary. There should be two at the start of each race, one to read out the names, and the other, if need be, to arrange the draw for position. Several more should be available to deal with the spectators, some of whom, if left to their own devices, will always contrive to be just where they are least wanted. It is a good plan to have lines drawn behind which the spectators must stand, and if reinforcements are necessary, old practice hurdles make a useful barrier.

Megaphonist and *Scorer*. There are also two other officials who are useful on the days of inter-school meetings or Sports finals. One is the megaphonist, who announces the results and times; the other the scorer, who chalks up the points on a black-board in a conspicuous position.

FIELD EVENTS. In the field events success, both from the spectators' and competitors' points of view, depends tremendously on the efficiency of the organization. Any kind of delay must be prevented if at all possible. It will perhaps be best to deal with each event separately.

High Jump. The High Jump needs four people to run it. One reads out the names, and if there be any delay by a competitor, he loses his turn; two more replace the cross-bar when needful, while a fourth rakes over the sand in the pit to keep it soft.

Long Jump. This event should also have four: one to call out the names and to watch the take-off board for "no jumps" (see A.A.A. Laws, p. 150); two more to measure each jump, one on either side of the pit (see Fig. 2 on p. 21); and a fourth to rake over the sand in the pit to keep it level and soft. Both for this event and also the Shot it is necessary to have a peg for each competitor with his name written on it to mark his best effort.

Putting the Shot. Four people are needed: one to call

Specimen cutting from score-sheets used in High Jump, Long Jump, and Shot Put

High Jump Open

Names	4·6	4·8	4·9	4·10	4·11
BROWN ...	✓	✓	××✓	×✓	×××
SMITH ...	×✓	✓	✓	✓	×✓
JONES ...	✓	×✓	×××✓	×××	

Long Jump Under 16 A

Names	1st	2nd	3rd
LAURIE ...	14·4	15·6	—
AMES ...	15·7	×No jump	15·10½
FLANAGAN	15·1¼	—	16·2¼

Shot Put Open

Names	1	2	3
JAMES ...	✓	—	✓
McCONNELL	✓	—	✓
MERCER ...	×No put	×No put	✓

Notes on symbols

✓ denotes successful effort.   × denotes a failure.   — denotes no improvement.

Fig. 3

out the names; another, who must have experience, to watch for "no puts" (see A.A.A. Laws, pp. 151–2); a third to mark each "put" with a peg; and a fourth to return the shot. In these last three events a piece of foolscap marked as in Fig. 3 and mounted on stout cardboard will be found most useful, especially in bad weather.

The Flat Events and their Staff-work

100 Yards. If possible, it is a good thing for the sprinters to dig their holes beforehand, so that the spectators are not kept waiting while excavations are in progress. Care should be taken that there is plenty of "worsted" at the winning-post, otherwise the whole meeting may be held up for lack of this essential, but inexpensive, material. The crowd should stand well back from the finish. I once saw a lady, who was meditating on the state of the weather, knocked down by one of the runners in whose path she had stepped at the end of the final of the Senior 100 Yards. Neither party was in the least pleased.

220 Yards. If it can be worked, this event should be run straight. If it is run round the track, it will have to be started in echelon; otherwise the runner drawing the outside place loses very heavily in the journey round the bend.

440 Yards. This race will profit by being started in echelon, with lanes ruled up to the first bend and round it, so that the runners are handicapped to equalize the draw round the first corner only (Fig. 4). By this means more runners can compete without fear of jostling, as by the time the corner is passed they will be strung out.

Half-Mile and *Mile.* At the end of each lap one of the time-keepers should shout out the time, so that the runners may know what speed they are making.

Hurdles. During the heats and when a relay race is being run, it is a time-saving device to have one or two boys stationed at each flight to pick up hurdles which have been knocked down.

Relay Races. During the sprint relay there should be a steward at each change-over station to see that the runners are ready and that the exchange is made correctly (see Rule on p. 148). Runners should be warned to be extremely careful not to cause obstruction when they have finished their stages, but to move off obliquely to the outside of the track.

THE TIME SCHEDULE

All big Sports meetings now have a fixed time-allowance for each event. The order will perhaps depend on the individual runners who are performing more than once, so that they may have as much rest in between their events as possible. The time allowed depends on the number of competitors in each event. The specimen programme given below, showing the finals of the School Sports as decided on two days, was actually finished a minute or two early on each day.

Events previously decided: Steeplechases, Senior and Junior; Putting the Shot, 440 Yards, and 220 Yards, Senior; Putting the Shot and Hurdles, Under 16; 220 Yards and High Jump, Under 15.

First Day

No.	Time	Event	Class	Number of competitors	Time allowed
1	2.30	High Jump	Under 16	6	15 mins.
2	2.45	Long Jump	Senior	6	15 ,,
3	3.0	Hurdles	Under 15	4	5 ,,
4	3.5	College Servants	(Race ½ mile)	—	10 ,,
5	3.15	440 Yards	Under 16	8	5 ,,
6	3.20	880 Yards	Senior	10	10 ,,
					Total 1 hr.

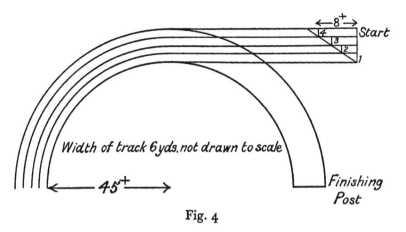

Width of track 6 yds. not drawn to scale

Start

Finishing Post

Fig. 4

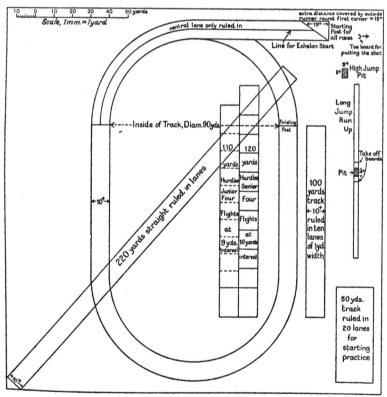

Scale, 1mm.=1yard

central lane only ruled in

Line for Echelon Start

extra distance covered by outside runner round first corner = 15 ft

Starting Post for all races

Toe board for putting the shot

High Jump Pit

Long Jump Run Up

Inside of Track, Diam. 90 yds

Finishing Post

220 yards straight ruled in lanes

110 yards / 120 yards

Hurdles Junior Four Flights at 9 yds. interval

Hurdles Senior Four Flights at 10 yards interval

Take off boards

Pit

100 yards track ruled in ten lanes of 1 yd width

50 yds. track ruled in 20 lanes for starting practice

Fig. 5

Shows a field marked out for the Sports. For want of space the lines behind which spectators should stand are not put in.

Second Day

No.	Time	Event	Class	Number of competitors	Time allowed
1	2.30	High Jump	Senior	6	15 mins.
2	2.45	100 Yards	Under 16	8	5 ,,
3	2.50	,,	Under 14	8	5 ,,
4	2.55	,,	Senior	8	5 ,,
5	3.0	Long Jump	Under 16	6	15 ,,
6	3.15	Old Boys	(Race 220 yards)	—	10 ,,
7	3.25	Hurdles	Senior	4	5 ,,
8	3.30	880 Yards	Under 16	8	5 ,,
9	3.35	1 Mile	Senior	8	10 ,,
					Total 1¼ hrs.

This programme is of course dependent on local conditions, such as the place of the Hurdles and Long Jump, which were the opposite side of the field from the finish of the other races. Spectators therefore must have time to move across and back again. The High Jump is often a protracted affair chiefly because the bar is put too low at the beginning. This is a matter of experience, but I should say the higher the better. In my opinion there should never be more than six competitors in the final of a field event, as even so it tends to become tedious for the spectators. At the same time it is absurd to think overmuch about making a "good show" of the Sports. It will be noticed that in the above programme the Senior Furlong and Quarter-Mile were run off previously. This was a deliberate effort to prevent boys doing too much on any one day, even at the expense of depriving the spectators of two good races to watch. I believe that two comparatively short programmes will make quite a "good enough show" so long as there is keen competition and good organization. So many meetings nowadays are much too long.

CHAPTER III

TRAINING FOR GENERAL FITNESS

THIS chapter deals with the attainment of physical fitness; for this is the first condition of success in any sphere of athletics, whether it be cross-country running or high jumping. How should a fellow set about this? Well, the first thing is to try to understand the main outlines of the problem, which is really a fascinating one when once you dip into it. So many go wrong in this matter because they will not bother to think for themselves. Instead, they either take second-hand advice which probably does not apply to them in the least, or else they shirk any kind of preparation altogether because "it is such a grind". The truth of the matter is that before embarking on a course of training you must understand what you are doing. Directly you attack the problem in an intelligent way, it will become interesting, and, with the entry of interest, boredom will fly out of the window.

You aim, then, at making your physical condition as perfect as possible, in order that your body may give of its best when called upon. By way of illustration let us imagine that you have the misfortune to possess a motor-bicycle, and are misguided enough to have entered for a hill-climbing competition. Under these circumstances you will want to know quite a lot about the engine of the infernal machine, and you will in all probability get very dirty "tuning it up". Likewise, surely common-sense dictates that, if you wish to produce the best results from your body, you must also try to understand something about its machinery in so far as it bears on the question in hand.

The machinery of the body is, of course, a highly

complex system, which it is extremely hard to describe in simple terms with anything like scientific accuracy. However, it seems to me that every athlete benefits so greatly from a knowledge of the outlines that I will try to sketch them as clearly as I can, avoiding technical terms wherever possible and confining myself to that which is important to athletics. The muscles, which move the various limbs, are made up of millions of tiny cells. These contract and expand on receiving messages flashed to them along the nerves from the brain. These muscles, in order to do their work efficiently, must be fed, and after each expenditure of energy need food for recovery; this they get in the form of fresh blood, which is pumped along the arteries by the heart. The amount of nourishment in the blood depends largely on how much oxygen it contains, and the process of oxygenating the blood is carried out by the lungs. The heart itself is a muscle, which expands and contracts like the other muscle cells, except that its action is continuous.

Up to a certain point the more work a muscle is given to do, the more efficient it becomes. It grows more elastic, and does more work on the same amount of oxygen. Suppose, for example, you go out for a training run. You are thereby exercising the muscles of your heart, lungs, and legs. If you do not overdo it, those muscles will have profited by their exercise in so far as they have gained elasticity, strength, and capacity for work. Your lungs likewise will have derived benefit by their more vigorous action and also will have supplied the rest of the body with a blood-stream more highly charged with oxygen. Hence the feeling of extreme health after vigorous, but not too vigorous, exercise. On the other hand, if you overdo things, *i.e.* push yourself along when your breath is whistling and your legs staggering, the result is the exact opposite. Instead of building up strength and stamina, you are simply breaking it down, so that a rest of several days will be necessary before you can carry on usefully with your training. The fitter you become as you carry on with your preparation, the stronger the action of the heart in sending a flow of vitalizing, oxygenated blood to the muscles as they work, and the more efficient the response of the muscles to the demand upon them.

Generally speaking, the difference between the physique of a man and that of a boy lies in the development of the heart muscle. If a man runs himself to a standstill, his legs give way before his heart and very little harm is done, as Nature has provided a safety-valve. A boy, however, *especially if he has not had sufficient training*, may run himself into a faint, which is definitely bad. Put rather crudely perhaps, this is the reason why I feel keen about boys getting sufficient "heart-training" to withstand the strain of vigorous racing.

This brings us to the question of Training. As I have said before, you must know what you are about and must try to tackle it scientifically. In order to do this, a return to the analogy of the motor-cycle may prove helpful. I think you will agree that, to have much chance of success and get the fullest satisfaction out of the game, you must first know a good deal about the engine of your monstrosity, and secondly do the "tuning up" with your own hands. There is a certain likeness between the motor-bicycle and the body of the athlete, but the pity of it is that so many leave the "tuning up" of their body either undone or in the hands of others.

How then can this "tuning up" process be best carried out for ourselves? There would seem to be four vital physical factors to be dealt with: (1) the heart, (2) the lungs, (3) the muscles, (4) the nervous system.

The last of these may sound a trifle odd. What I mean is this. It is no good having the most perfectly trained body in every other respect if there is no force to drive the machine. This power is, in the final consideration, a matter of mind. If a runner is mentally stale or, to put it colloquially, "fed up with the whole show", however physically fit he may be, he will never succeed in any sphere of athletics, as he will lack "drive" and the co-ordination between mind and muscle will be faulty. There are two common ways of falling victim to this curse. One is by a system of training either overdone or so lacking in variety as to tire the mind; the other is by overdoing the competition, which is a considerable strain on the nervous system. Sometimes boys, or for that matter even experienced men, do not realize when they are suffering from mental staleness. But if you feel listless and, seemingly for no reason, cannot produce your correct form, even though you may not actually dislike your event and everything connected with it, you may take it for granted that you are mentally stale. The only remedy, really, is rest with plenty of fresh air and walks.

THE HEART. The heart-training of which I have spoken can, in my opinion, be carried out best by jog-trotting over distances from a mile and upwards—how far you go will depend on what event you wish to train for especially. This jog-trotting is essentially a slow business, very little faster than a brisk walk, i.e. about $2\frac{1}{2}$ to $3\frac{1}{2}$ minutes to each quarter-mile. You plod along on the flats of the feet, and do not be afraid of making a noise, as the jarring, flat-footed action in itself does good by shaking up and loosening the muscles.

This action is called a "shack", deriving from the ponderous trotting of a cart-horse. It is, to my mind, a first-class exercise for toning up the heart and lungs at the beginning of training; the distances should be gradually increased, but *the speed should remain the same*. Its great merit is that it does its work slowly without causing undue exhaustion. Days off football at the beginning of the term are the time for the "shack". Begin with a mile and increase by half a mile at a time—it does not matter where you go, though preferably it should be level. When you have done a certain amount of "shacking", but not before, you can get on to the faster work; "shacking", however, or its equivalent, is essential as a beginning. For those whose time is limited, slow skipping also is admirable both for heart and lungs, especially if done in the open air. This, however, should not be overdone, as violent skipping at a fast rate is one of the most vigorous forms of exercise you can take.

THE LUNGS. The lungs, of course, benefit from the "shack" and any form of wise exercise that you take. Breathing exercises, if possible in front of an open window, are excellent. The following are recommended: (1) Take in a deep breath through the nose from the stomach, pushing it out as far as it will go. Hold it for a few seconds, then expel forcefully through the mouth, at the same time pressing the stomach inwards till you have driven every particle of air out of your lungs. Do this two or three times. (2) Fill the lungs as full as you can, as above; then, still holding your breath, draw in your stomach as far as possible several times. This exercise drives the fresh air into the upper portions of the lungs which are not generally used, except in vigorous exercise, thus tending to collect the waste products of the breath.

THE MUSCLES. When a man is running, hurdling, or doing any other form of athletics, his efficiency will depend to a tremendous extent on the way in which he has trained his muscles. If I go out and take vigorous exercise to which I am not accustomed, I am very stiff in the muscles which did the work. That stiffness is caused by the unfitness of those particular muscles. I may, for instance, be very fit for a hard game of football; but if I were to turn out on the track and run an "all out" furlong without having done any track work beforehand, you may be sure that the next day would find me with the muscles at the back of my thighs—the chief sprinting muscles—quite unpleasantly sore to the touch. How bad they are will depend on whether I have taken any trouble over my muscular condition. There will always be a certain amount of "soreness" when work on the track is begun, but this may be cut down to a minimum and in addition the efficiency of the muscles considerably increased by the man who is keen enough to carry out a certain number of exercises. The ideal, of course, is to keep your muscular system in such condition that you can turn out and take any form of vigorous exercise with a minimum of after-effects.

The following list of exercises is big enough to give plenty of variety, which is most desirable in order to avoid boredom. It also brings into play all the muscles which are most important to the athlete. Remember that three or four minutes of exercises before roosting each evening is quite enough, but you *must* be regular. Forming the habit may be tiresome, but once formed it becomes automatic.

Exercise	*Notes*
(1) Touching the toes with the knuckles or palms of the hands, keeping the knees well braced back. (Figs. 6 and 7)	Back of thighs and calves
(2) Knee-lifting. Standing on one leg, lift the knee of the other towards the chin 6 to 12 times	Front of thighs. Good for balance
(3) High kicking. Every athlete should be able to kick his own height. Do No. 1 first and begin not too energetically, taking care not to sit down backwards	Back of thighs and hips

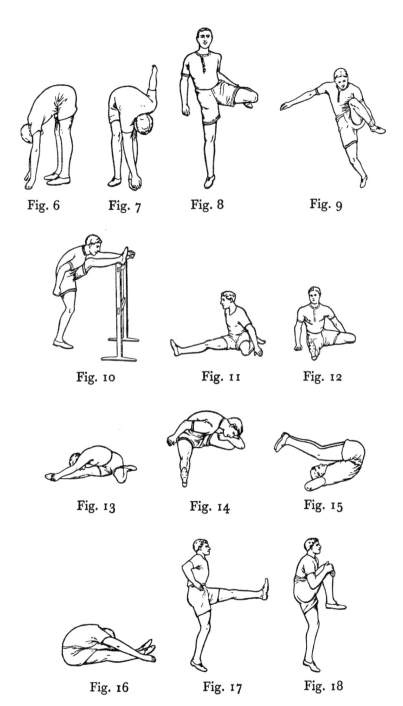

Fig. 6   Fig. 7   Fig. 8   Fig. 9

Fig. 10   Fig. 11   Fig. 12

Fig. 13   Fig. 14   Fig. 15

Fig. 16   Fig. 17   Fig. 18

Exercise	*Notes*
(4) Pick up knee as in Fig. 8 and swing it forwards and upwards for as long a stride as possible (see Fig. 9). To add to the interest, measure the distance. Not to be done more than two or three times.	Chiefly to make hips flexible
(5) Resting the heel on some support 3 ft. to 3½ ft. high, stretch forwards and downwards till you touch the knee with your chin. N.B. The knees of both legs must be well braced back. (See Fig. 10)	Back of thighs
(6) Take up the hurdling position on the floor, as in Figs. 11 and 12. The thighs should be at right-angles and the body absolutely upright. Having got the position correctly (which with some people may take time), stretch forward as in Fig. 13. When you have mastered this, try to run the elbow round the knee of the back leg (see Fig. 14). This is not easy and will hurt, but with some practice quite a number of boys can do it. Nos. 4 and 5 should always precede 6	The best exercise for all-round suppleness; useful for every athletic event, though mostly used for hurdling
(7) Lie on the back and raise both legs together slowly up and down without actually resting them on the ground (see Fig. 15). Six times should be the maximum	Stomach muscles, which are most important in every event
(8) Lie on back and raise body, stretching forward till chin touches knees, six times as above. Nos. 7 and 8 are alternate—or rather, never do more than three of each at a time. (Fig. 16)	As above

Exercise	Notes
(9) The ordinary P.T. "knees bend" is excellent for the instep and ankles, but you must keep well up on the tips of the toes as you do it. When you can do it nicely on both legs, try doing it on each singly with the other held out stiffly in front of you	A general leg-strengthener
(10) Raising one leg stiffly to the front, hop lightly on the other leg 6 to 12 times (Fig. 17). Another useful variation of this exercise is to do it with the knee flexed and raised as far as possible towards the chin	Knee-lift and in-step-balance
(11) Taking hold of the knee, as in Fig. 18, and raising it well up, poise yourself on the toe of the other leg and reach out for as long a stride as you can	As above
(12) "Press-ups" from the fingers, not the palms of the hands. This strengthens the arms and fingers for the crouch start and shot-put	—
(13) Stand with feet well apart and hands locked behind neck. Then do a series of movements from the waist. Bending forward with a good straight back; twisting to right and left and bending backwards keeping the chin well drawn in. This is of course really a P.T. exercise and does not need details	General flexibility of the muscles of the trunk
(14) Stand with the feet 14 inches apart and do the sprinting arm action without moving the legs (see Chap. iv, pp. 56–57)	—

Note on Exercises. Be very careful not to overdo these exercises. If you feel tired for an hour after them, or cannot sleep, you will know that you have done too much; in which case you will have broken down rather than built up. The best plan is to take half a dozen exercises and do a few of each rather than concentrate on one or two.

There is a very common mistake about muscles. It is widely thought that it is of the utmost importance to have big, hard muscles. Certainly this is true in that muscles, when contracted, should be firm and bulging; but it is equally essential that they should be soft and pliable when at rest. Exercises such as the above are mostly of the stretching, loosening variety, but many people who are naturally muscular need massage as well in order to get absolutely free from all stiffness.

The importance of pliable muscles is hard to exaggerate. Not only do people with hard, lumpy muscles thereby spoil the efficiency of their performances very considerably, but also they lay themselves open to some form of muscular breakdown. This applies mostly to sprinters, hurdlers, jumpers, and shot-putters, whose movements are sudden and violent. The calves and thighs are particularly liable to give trouble. Prevention is of course infinitely superior to cure, and is, moreover, generally quite possible if, before competing, a series of stretching exercises is always run through—any of the first six in the above list are first-rate for this purpose. Should the weather be very cold, it is a good plan to rub the legs with some kind of grease or embrocation, especially for cross-country work.

A certain amount of self-massage can be given to the legs. The muscles should be picked up in the fingers, drawn away from the bone, and any hard lumps kneaded out; finish with a brisk rub over the surface of the skin from the ankles upwards. The idea of massage is to loosen up the muscle fibres and promote a free circulation of blood. It is not within the province of this book to deal with the treatment of muscular strains and sprains; at the same time it is urged that the policy of leaving the trouble to mend itself may result in a weakness in that limb for life.

THE PROBLEM OF FOOD. One of the questions which I am always being asked is about the best kind of diet. Frankly I should say "Do not bother about it". Eat ordinary every-day food and *chew it up thoroughly*. If not, you are imposing a strain on your interior man which is hardly fair on him; you also risk carrying about an uncomfortable and unnecessary passenger in the form of undigested food. Generally speaking, it is a mistake to eat between meals, as the stomach objects to odd jobs and prefers to do its work in one piece, so that it may enjoy its rest. If you *must* visit the tuck-shop, I should strongly advise you to invest in fruit rather than in sweets, though plain chocolate is all right in moderation.

Do not get it into your head that you should starve in training. Generally the more physical exercise a man takes, the more food he eats, or should eat (whether he has eaten too much is a matter of which each must judge for himself). As a matter of fact it is not unusual to put *on* weight in training, probably because you are making muscle, which is heavier than fat.

The only time when it is wise to be careful about your food and drink is on the day of a race. It is, I think, a fairly generally accepted fact that digestive processes are improved by drinking between rather than at meals. Also it should be remembered that the most easily digested foodstuffs take two hours to be assimilated, while the least take over four hours. The moral is: feed light just before running, giving a miss to potatoes, new bread, and such-like heavy stuff. Concentrate therefore on a good breakfast on that day instead, and drink in the middle of the morning instead of at lunch.

THE ENEMIES OF SUCCESSFUL TRAINING. Now I shall deal with some of the factors which prevent perfect fitness.

Teeth and Tonsils. Just before the Olympic Games in 1924 I had rather an unpleasant muscular breakdown. The pain was considerable, and I was most anxious about my chances for the Games. I therefore went straight off to a big muscle specialist in Harley Street. His first question was: "Are your tonsils all right? And have you had your teeth overhauled lately?" These seemed to me, then, rather irrelevant questions. I now know that septic tonsils or an abscess in the mouth, even though not especially noticeable under ordinary conditions, will poison the blood system in such a way that a man will be extremely liable to muscle trouble. Reference to p. 34 will show how this can be. If therefore your teeth are wrong or you are continually having a sore throat, it will be a strategic move to have things put right, quite apart from any considerations of athletics.

Colds. Nurmi, the Finn, did break a world's record with a cold on him, but to the ordinary being a chill has a devastating effect, as it not only spoils the wind, but considerably lowers vitality. Here again "prevention is better than cure", and I will make a suggestion which, however, I fear few will be wise enough to adopt. Apart from breathing exercises, which are excellent, the best way of safeguarding yourself against colds, or any other disease of a like nature, is to gargle and sniff up each nostril some disinfectant such as glyco-thymolin or peroxide of hydrogen suitably mingled with water. This should be done night and morning; takes two minutes; is horrible at first, but quite easy when the habit is formed.

If you have actually got a cold, there are certain

remedies which I have found helpful for myself, though it does not at all follow that everyone else will benefit from them. They are a glass of hot lemonade, plus 5 to 10 grains of aspirin, the last thing at night; sleep with a sweater on, scarf round the neck and socks on the feet—this is extremely unpleasant, but tends to deal with the situation adequately. "Vapex" or some such preparation on the pillow by night and on the handkerchief by day is also helpful.

If you feel a cold coming on, in its earliest stages it may be driven off by quinine. It is, however, a mistake to take quinine when the cold has hold of you, as it does not really cure, but merely prolongs it. The best stuff to take when you have a cold is, in my experience, "Sirop Famel", a French preparation.

Hot Baths. The greatest giver of colds, to my mind, is the hot bath. Boys will wallow in a bath with the temperature at about 110° F. for half an hour or so, if they are lucky enough (as they think) to get one. They then stand about in draughts with their pores well open and grouse because they have streaming colds next day. Hot baths are all too pleasant, but, so far as physical fitness is concerned, pernicious. Such a bath, besides its cold-giving qualities, takes the "snap" out of the muscles for, perhaps, two or three days after. If you *must* have a hot bath, you can set things right by (1) having a cold shower or bath afterwards, or (2) letting in cold water till the water is something cooler than tepid. If you do this, you will guard against cold by closing the pores; moreover you will brace the muscles again to a certain extent at least. And this brings me to the subject of cold baths in the morning.

Cold Baths. There is a good deal of controversy about their effect on health and it is impossible to generalize. A friend of mine, himself a doctor and athlete, is a great upholder of the cold bath as a means to healthfulness.

The whole question depends on your reaction to the cold water. If you do not feel warmth irradiating your body afterwards, but are inclined to shiver, it will be best to warm the water somewhat. Personally I think that as a preventive of colds and a promoter of fitness for those who can stand them, there are few things better than a cold bath. It is a great advantage also to give yourself a rub down with the palms of the hands immediately after. Brisk friction over the surface of the skin, from the extremities towards the heart, brings a most pleasant glow of health, which I think is itself sufficient argument in its favour.

Constipation. This is another enemy of mankind in general, though it *should* not trouble the athlete who is looking after himself. At least one regular action each day is essential, preferably two. At the least signs of a falling off in this respect, prompt steps should be taken. Tasteless paraffin is excellent, as it has no chemical effects on the body. Kruschen and Eno's Salts are stronger in their effects; but the thing to remember is that, however you deal with the situation, constipation *must* not be neglected at any time and especially not when in training.

Smoking. Here we have another splendid bone of contention, which *should* not affect boys at school. Medical opinions of course differ in this matter, though most doctors would condemn the habit in boys who are still developing physically. Personally I look at it this way. When I smoke a cigarette, whether I inhale or not, I absorb into my blood a certain amount of stuff which is certainly not helpful, and in large quantities is definitely harmful. I myself have never smoked very much, nor have my friends who have been most successful with their running. But suppose I have two cigarettes a day, the cost may be perhaps a lowering of efficiency by 1 per cent. or perhaps a yard or two in a quarter-mile. Well,

I want that extra bit badly enough to think it not worth while risking it in a rather silly way.

It is of course a question which each must decide for himself. Some very successful athletes have played fast and loose with themselves without immediate, apparent loss of proficiency. But I believe that they inevitably pay for it later on in life, and also that they would probably have done even better had they been kinder to their bodies.

Before ending this chapter it will be well to touch on the question of leaving off training. The temptation to do so suddenly is naturally pretty strong. But this is a great mistake and is responsible for the premature end of many athletic careers as well as a break-up in general health in many cases. Every fellow ought to keep himself fit all the year round, both in holidays and term-time, by more or less vigorous exercise. To put it in another way, there should not be a very big margin between being "in training", *i.e.* tuned up for racing, and merely in decent physical condition. Personally I run a mile at "shack" pace every morning and do some skipping before breakfast; and although at times it is a bore, I believe it is infinitely worth it.

So far I have kept fairly close to the subject of health and athletics. But this general fitness training, if carried out in the right spirit, has two results which are much wider and more important. In the first place you learn how to look after yourself physically, which is an asset to any human being. Secondly, you raise your body to a higher plane of physical fitness and will taste of that wonderful *joie de vivre* when you want to jump over the moon from sheer excess of vitality and animal spirits. I sometimes think that it is worth while going into training for that alone.

CHAPTER IV

THE TECHNIQUE OF RUNNING, WITH SOME
SUGGESTIONS FOR TRAINING
ON THE TRACK

Does a man run entirely by the light of nature, or is it an art in any way comparable with swimming, golf, or cricket, which can definitely be learnt by those who want to do so? Put in a nutshell: is there anything *in* running that can be picked up either from a coach or from the printed page? Such are the questions which I hope to answer definitely and affirmatively in this chapter.

The very seeming simplicity of running is itself a snare; yet when the crack runner who has style is seen alongside of the novice, the contrast is so marked that perhaps some may wonder where the difference between them lies. "What is this style?" they may ask. "It looks well and certainly seems effective." Now as a matter of fact there are, to my mind, two different styles in running, both of which should be at the command of every runner. One is the striding and the other the sprinting style, both of which I shall discuss in detail later.

For the moment let us consider the basic principles which any particular style must obey if it claim to be really effective: (1) The arms, legs, and body must all work together smoothly and harmoniously in such a way as to produce maximum speed for the amount of energy expended. (2) Every time a muscle in any part of the body is contracted, it uses up a certain store of the energy. Therefore it is essential that in running only those muscles which are really effective in propelling the body along should be used—that is to say, that any undue tightening up of other parts of the body, unnecessary to the running action, not only is a waste of energy but also will very probably add to the exertion by upsetting balance and by pulling against the muscles which are doing their work correctly. (3) The body itself is, as it were, a passenger, whose business it should be to make things as easy as possible for the legs and arms, its steed. A jockey's chief ambition is to get his weight as far forward as possible, and indeed a forward lean, slight or emphasized according to the length of the race, is one of the most important assets to any running style. (4) Lastly, an essential of smooth economical action lies in perfect poise and balance.

To summarize: any runner who would consider his style scientifically must satisfy himself that he has unity of action, *i.e.* legs, arms, and body working together; that he is not throwing away energy unnecessarily; that his body carriage is correct, and that he has balance.

THE STRIDING ACTION. Now I will analyse in detail the striding action which in my opinion seems to satisfy the principles given above. It will be easiest for this purpose to split it up into the functions of the legs, arms, and body.

The legs. Perhaps the first thing to do in criticizing a striding action is to use your ears. Very often you will hear a heavy, thudding sound. Ideally when striding a man should run so lightly as to be almost noiseless; in other words, the action should be full of spring from the balls of the feet. The shorter the distance, the more will he get up on his toes, while in the longer races, *i.e.* anything over a mile, the heel may just touch the ground. This "foot action" depends on the strength of the ankle and instep and is extremely important, as it gives "zip" to the whole movement, just as a flick of the wrist lends speed to the ball at cricket. It is moreover a point of weakness with many boys, who have a tendency to plod along on the flats of their feet. Much can be done to develop the ankles and insteps by exercises Nos. 9 and 10 (see p. 41).

B   4

Another leg action fault, which is by no means confined to novices, is the kick-up behind. Ideally the leg from which the stride is taken should come straight through for the next stride without flick-up behind. Very often it is the most successful runners who are the worst offenders in this respect. The reason is that the stronger the leg action the greater the liability to flick up at the conclusion of the stride, rather in the same way as certain batsmen with good wrists are inclined to over-flourish. A fault, however, it is, in that both time and energy are wasted thereby, and every effort should be made to get out of it. This may be done best in practice by cultivating an exaggerated knee-lift in front, rather like a trotting horse. It has also the advantage of lengthening the stride (see exercises 2, 10, 11, 12 on pp. 39–41). There are, in fact, two ways of doing this, the first and best as suggested above, while the other depends on a swing from the hips plus a stretch out with the fore-leg. The danger of this latter method is that in straightening out the fore-leg there is a strong tendency for the body to get too much upright instead of having a forward lean. Actually in each stride the weight of the body should be well forward over the front leg as it comes to the ground. It is not difficult to know for yourself when this is so by the sensation of balance and by the ease with which you move along.

A long stride is of course far from being everything, but if you can train your muscles to give you an inch or so on to your stride without any more conscious effort by yourself it will be worth while. Let us suppose that you are a half-miler and that your natural stride is 6 ft. By developing your knee-lift and hip action you manage to add 2 in. to that stride; that is to say that in a given time, say 2 minutes, you get in the same number of strides without exhausting yourself any more. When your stride was 6 ft., *i.e.* 2 yards, you took about 440 strides. With the added 2 in. per stride in 2 minutes you will cover 880 yards + (440 × 2) inches, *i.e.* about 25 yards, representing a gain of some 4 seconds on your half-mile time. This may seem an extreme example of theory, but it does actually happen; and if you remember this when you are training it will have a most cheering effect, especially when it is difficult to summon enough energy to carry on. I could as a matter of fact name a dozen runners straight off who have improved themselves almost incredibly, sheerly by taking trouble, and some of them seemed the very reverse of promising material in the first place.

Fig. 19   Fig. 20

The arms. But this is a digression; let me return to the question of arm action, about which there is so much controversy. There are in this matter two schools of thought, one of which favours a swing across the body while the other supports the backwards and forwards movement. Personally I compromise. For the *striding action* which I am now discussing I believe that the hands should be lightly clenched and the swing diagonally across the body, but never further than the centre of it. The elbows should be bent at an angle of about 90° (see Figs. 19 and 20). Very little muscular effort goes into the arm action when striding; the swing should go with the movement of the shoulders and there should be a slight emphasis on the forward movement. Care should be taken not to allow the hands to fly out sideways further than the hips.

The essence of the matter is that the whole of the upper part of the body should be perfectly loose and relaxed. The reason for the diagonal arm swing is that it keeps the muscles of the chest free from tension and thereby eases the work of the lungs. Moreover the fact that there is no drive in the arm action prevents the tendency towards a sideway roll and consequent loss of balance.

The body. The trunk plays a passive part in the operation, but it is nevertheless of great importance that its angle should be correct. As the stride begins and just before the take-off foot leaves the ground, there should be a straight line from the heel to the back of the head. The whole body has then gone into the stride, straightening out with a flick like a piece of steel which has been bent double.

Now this straight line is a fundamental of good striding action, as is also the forward lean of the body. Some coaches, however, will tell you that you should lean forward from the waist. But if you do this it is obvious that you must break the straight line and lose power thereby. The true way of insuring a good body-angle is to adjust your length of stride in such a way that the weight of your body is always well over your front foot as it comes to the ground. Should you be striding too long for your strength, you reach out to your front foot ahead of you and drag your body along in an upright position. Some runners find it a comparatively easy matter to keep their weight forward, but others, the heavy-weights with big shoulders in particular, find it a continual source of difficulty, especially at the end of a race when they are tiring and every instinct urges a longer stride in order to gain ground.

In this connection it is interesting to take the evidence

of the slow-motion cinema camera which takes 200 ex-
posures per second. At a fast quarter-mile stride 60
photos were taken to one stride, *i.e.* from the moment
when one foot touched the ground to the moment when
the other did so. Of these, 30 were taken while the body
was in the air and 30 when a foot was on the ground; in
other words, the whole stride of just over 8 ft. took
30/100 sec. It is surprising to find how long the feet
spend in contact with the ground, and if it is possible
to cut that time down by even the smallest fraction of a
second without loss of stride-length it will be a definite
gain. But, as I have pointed out above, that time is
largely determined by the fore-leg stretch. The further
it reaches out to the front, the longer will it take to drag
the body forward for the next stride. Conversely, the
more forward is the body over the front foot, the less
tractive work has the foot to do and the quicker it does
it. Enough should have been said to show the importance
of body-angle and its connection with stride-lengths. The
problem in sprinting is somewhat different, as will be
shown later.

The head. Not without importance also is carriage of
the head. Its action is that of a rudder and it should
always be held level, with the eyes looking straight
ahead. There are two bad mistakes which are made, I
suppose, at every athletic meeting. A very large number
of runners cannot resist the temptation of looking over
their shoulder "to see how the other chaps are getting
on". Have you ever noticed that even when you are
walking and try to look behind you, your feet fall over
each other? Well, if you do this when you are running,
especially when you are tired, it is fairly obvious that
your stride will be shortened and your balance upset.
Therefore you should always avoid it unless you are
certain that you have a huge lead and want to save
yourself as much as possible. Many races have been lost

even by experienced runners who are "pipped on the tape" through looking round.

The other fault, which has even worse consequences, lies in throwing the chin up and the head back. The temptation to do so in an exhausting race is very great, but it cannot be too severely checked. When once the head goes back, the body almost automatically becomes upright and the muscles of the chest tighten up, thereby interfering with the free action of the lungs. Here, then, you have a vicious circle. As you tire, you let your head go back, and this contracts unnecessary muscles, hinders breathing, and causes further fatigue. Therefore I say again that, however weary you are, you must concentrate on keeping your head level and the muscles of your neck and chest relaxed.

So much then for the analysis of the striding action. Now comes the question of when it is used, and the answer is simple—in the middle stages of all races over 100 yards where speed goes hand in hand with economy of effort.

THE SPRINT ACTION. The chief difference between the sprinting and the striding action is that in the latter the runner wants to cover the ground at a good pace, but not so fast as to leave him without strength for the decisive effort at the finish; in sprinting, speed and liveliness of movement are the essentials and the question of saving energy does not arise.

The problem really lies in applying your whole strength so skilfully that it is all transformed into speed over the ground. The novice who has plenty of strength so often runs as one beating the air, and the harder he struggles the slower he goes. The difficulty for the majority of sprinters is not so much lack of power as of ability to put the strength they have effectively into their running.

The action which I am about to detail is such that anyone, however slow he may be, can learn it and add to his speed thereby. Moreover it is my belief that every type of runner ought to make a point of mastering this style, even if he be exclusively a long-distance man. I have known at least one boy who improved his time for the Mile by upwards of 20 seconds in a year largely by developing his sprinting powers on these lines.

Many of the canons of striding apply equally to sprinting, but there are certain differences.

The legs. The leg action has not so much of the bounding spring. It is more pounding, with emphasis on the downward stamp and the drive off the back leg. In order to get the necessary downward drive it is essential to cultivate a good knee-lift. The stride also must be shortened a few inches by clipping in the fore-leg. The reason for this is obvious, especially in the light of the experiment with the slow-motion camera cited above; for if the full stride be taken, too much time is spent in the air and the liveliness essential to the true spring action is lost. This shortening of the stride is all-important, but is not at all easy to manage successfully, as the strides are liable to become irregular. Considerable practice is needed to set this right, but I am certain that it is infinitely worth it. One sprinter, almost entirely owing to this, improved his performance in the 100 Yards by $\frac{3}{10}$ second in one summer, thereby raising himself into the top flight of the world's sprinters instead of being an ordinary class performer.

It has been said above that the leg action is more pounding and less springing than striding. This is true, but it must not be thought that the expression "pounding" means anything flat-footed. As a matter of fact the sprinter should be always well forward on his toes; the heel should never touch the ground from start to finish of a sprint race.

The arms. The question of arm action is a vexed one between the "across-the-body" and the "backwards-

and-forwards" partisans. In this case I am a firm upholder of the latter. *The* great difference between sprinting
and striding lies in the arm action. When striding there is
little or no drive with the arms, which swing with the
rhythm of the body, but in sprinting the arms come
vigorously into play.

Now to my mind it is impossible to get a maximum
leverage with the arms when they swing across the body.
If you really drive hard with the arms in this way,
the tendency to throw yourself off balance is so great
that you either develop a lateral roll, which must detract

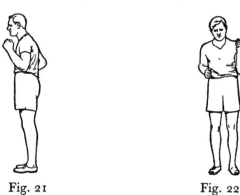

Fig. 21   Fig. 22

from the liveliness of your running, or else you waste
precious energy in counteracting it and thus lose power.
Actually I believe that those who preach this method
very rarely practise it in competition. The faster they
have to go, the more their arms swing diagonally backwards and forwards instead of across.

The action which I strongly recommend for the great
majority is as follows. The hands should be lightly
clenched as in striding; the elbows, however, should be
more flexed, at about 75°–80°, so that the swing shall
be a shorter one in keeping with the clipped stride (see
Figs. 21 and 22). The movement is straight "fore and
aft"; the hands must not rise above shoulder height nor
go farther back than the level of the hips, the elbows being

kept well into the sides. Now comes the important part to remember. There should be no emphasis whatever on the upward and forward swing; all the drive is put into the downward and backward pull which governs the downward drive of the leg action.

In any hard-fought race there is always a danger of allowing the hands to fly upwards. If this happens, the head goes back and at once you have one of the worst running faults. Now it is a favourite argument against this form of action that there is a special tendency for the arms to go up; but it is an objection raised more especially by those who have not studied the action closely. For *so long as the downward and backward pull is emphasized*, there is no danger that the hands will fly *up*, though it is possible that they may go a trifle too far *back*. This, however, may be counteracted quite easily by keeping the hands well into the sides, with the knuckles turned outwards, as they naturally do. It may also be found that the pull of the right hand tends to exceed that of the left. The result of uneven arm action is likely to produce an uneven stride and, if it be very pronounced, will cause a galloping movement off the stronger leg. The loss of smoothness and harmony in the action is serious and should be watched for in practice. By dint of laying stress on the left arm pull it can soon be set right. Lastly, be very careful not to let the arms and shoulders tighten up; however hard you are working them, the muscles should always be loose, and indeed the more relaxed they are the more quickly and vigorously will the arms do their work.

The body. All the remarks about body-angle in striding hold good here, except that the lean should be more exaggerated—in fact, a forward body-angle is one of the first essentials in sprinting, hence one of the chief reasons for the shortened stride. It is indeed so obvious as to be hardly worth labouring that, if the body has a falling forward tendency, the work of the legs and arms will be infinitely easier than if it is in an erect or backward position. At the same time this will probably be found the most difficult matter for the novice, as the vigorous action of the legs makes the forward lean extremely hard to hold.

THE USE OF THE SPRINT ACTION. I have said that all runners ought to master the technique of sprinting before they can count themselves polished performers. It follows, then, that this action is by no means confined to runners of the Hundred, and as a matter of fact it can be used with advantage twice at least, and often three or four times, in *any* race over 100 yards. First, then, runners should start every race, even cross-country, in this style. To go all out for the first 40 or 50 yards is extremely sound policy because (*a*) it raises the speed of the heart-beat, thereby insuring an adequate blood-stream to feed the muscles, and incidentally hastening the arrival of the second wind, which is largely a matter of the system adjusting itself to the demands upon it; (*b*) it does not tire you, as might be thought, but works off the accumulation of nervous energy which is generally called "wind up"; (*c*) it gathers momentum and gets you well into your stride; (*d*) it will often give you the inside berth at the first corner, coupled with a useful lead over the slower starters.

Secondly, if you wish to pass an opponent, you must always aim to "shoot" him by a sudden spurt. Here, then, again the sprint action, even for three or four strides, is advantageous.

Thirdly, you should cultivate it for the finish, which is undoubtedly the most important part of any race; moreover it is just here that this style has its greatest use. I have often heard it urged that the stride should be lengthened at the finish. This sounds admirable, but is, I believe, not practicable for any but the genius. The fact of the matter is that the harder you try to lengthen your stride when you are tiring, the more upright will your body become, thus making the work of the legs harder just when they are least able to meet the demand upon them. To my mind there is not the least doubt that the sprint action, with its quicker, shorter stride plus the forward body-lean and auxiliary driving force of the arms, more than outweighs the few inches loss in stride-length. The effect of slipping from the stride into the sprint is very much the same as changing gear in a car when sudden acceleration is needed at low speeds. Moreover it is possible that there is the added gain in that the sprinting action brings into play muscles which are comparatively fresh, giving thereby a new lease of life to the runner.

EXERCISES FOR THE IMPROVEMENT
OF TECHNIQUE

The practice stride action. This is simply the striding action as detailed, *but with every point slightly accentuated, i.e.* spring off the ball of the foot, knee-lift, body well forward, forward swing of arms, head level, relaxation of muscles in the upper part of the body. There is of course no attempt at economy, as in competition striding. When you are fairly satisfied with your attempts at the above, try running down a line keeping your strides just on either side of it. This is not easy, but is quite excellent for giving balance.

The practice sprint action. Carry out the action as described, but do not try to make any speed, concentrating entirely on correct form. This will give you the "feel" of the action, which must become so much a habit that you will never have to bother about it in competition. The great principle in learning to sprint is never to run so fast that you feel yourself losing balance and control of arms and legs. Directly this happens you must ease your efforts, as at the moment when you begin to lose form you will also lose speed, and the more you fight the slower you will go. It has often been found that when two champion sprinters meet in competition, the time is slower than that which they can each do when not so pressed; and the reason is simply that, in their fear of each other, they become rattled and fail to hold their form.

Cornering is a stumbling-block for many runners. If therefore your distance is short enough to warrant your taking corners at speed, you should try to perfect yourself in rounding them with as little loss of speed as possible. The great secret of this is to lean well over inwards (see Plate II). The sharper the bend the more the lean, and indeed there should be few corners, however abrupt, that cannot be taken at full speed so long as the surface is firm. The best practice for this is to run round a corner actually on the line. This will teach you not to swing outwards, which is a bad fault.

In the analysis of the striding action I suggested that if the legs could be trained to produce a bigger stride with the same amount of effort, the result would be well worth having. The two exercises which I am about to suggest will do much towards developing the necessary muscles to increase the stride output. At the same time it must be emphasized that they are both extremely vigorous and will only be useful if taken in small doses. There are two methods of making your natural striding capacity greater, first by a bigger knee-lift and secondly a more flexible hip action plus a fore-leg stretch.

If you want to learn anything well, you must exaggerate it; hence these exercises.

(a) Keeping the body slightly bent forward from the waist, run with quite a short stride, but with the knee-lift as big as possible, aiming as though to hit your chin with each knee (see Fig. 23).

PLATE II

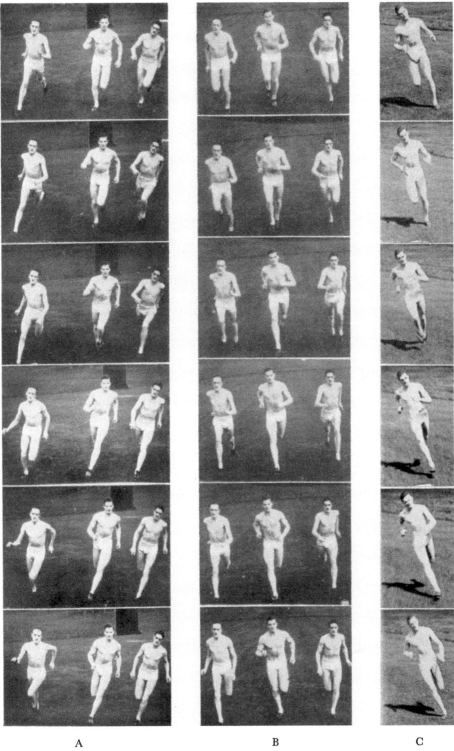

A	B	C

ILLUSTRATING THE INWARD LEAN WHEN CORNERING

In A the runner on the inside, Lowe, is taking a sharper bend than the other two so that he is leaning over more than them. Stallard on the outside is running rather wider than he need, probably through not leaning sufficiently inward. Series B is put in largely to provide a contrast from A and C. Here the runners are striding down the straight. Incidentally the arm action should be noted. As it should be when striding there is no drive in it, the arms swinging with the movement of the shoulders and slightly across the body. In C the runner is taking an abrupt corner at a good pace so that the inward lean is much more exaggerated.

(*b*) Run with the knees braced well back and a long exaggerated swing from the hips; the arms to balance this long stride effort are swung from the shoulders and unflexed at the elbows as seen in Fig. 24. It will be found that, if done properly, 20 strides, *i.e.* 10 off each leg, will be quite enough to begin with, and it is definitely inadvisable ever to do more than 50 of either at a stretch.

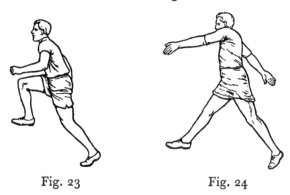

Fig. 23   Fig. 24

SOME GENERALIZATIONS ABOUT TRAINING

A runner who is training for a race wants two things, stamina and speed. Some want more of one than the other and should arrange their programme of work accordingly. It seems impossible to suggest a definite scheme of training; the differences of physique and circumstances are so varied that I consider it better to give principles on which schemes can be built up by each runner for himself.

Here, then, are some basic principles which apply to all running; for details of each event look at the next chapter. The work must be divided into that which aims at producing stamina and that which develops speed.

For stamina you should run distances half as much again, or double, that for which you especially wish to train, at quarter to three-quarter speed (see Tables, p. 67). Start with the long distances at slow speeds and work up to the shorter distances at a brisker pace. Do not run full-speed trials over the distance of your race. This is exhausting and rarely helpful, unless you are training over a long period and cannot get races in competition. To strengthen the legs the knee-lift and hip-swing striding exercises are first-rate.

Do not forget that you aim at building up strength and endurance. The worst fault and the most common among all types of athlete is "over-training". A very sound method of guarding against this danger is to remember that at the end of each day's outing you should feel like doing it again after an hour's rest. In other words, never should you be "done to the world" after training—or for that matter after racing, if your preparation has been right. If you *do* feel so, it simply means that you have been breaking down instead of building up your physique.

For speed. So long as it is not overdone, starting-practice up to 40 or 50 yards is excellent. To develop the ability to spurt quickly, move round the track at half-speed stride and alternate with short bursts of sprinting, being especially careful to hold your form. The best way to cultivate a finish is to run half the distance of your event at the correct speed, breaking into the sprint action for the last 15 yards. This may be lengthened by 5 to 10 yards at a time till you can master the finish which you decide best for yourself.

Pace-judgment may be combined with the last exercise when you are aiming to run half the distance of your race at the correct speed (see speed tables, Chapter vi). Get a friend to time you and note your error at each attempt, together with the weather conditions. Never lose a chance of learning your own speed, as it is one of the first marks of a skilful performer that he has an almost uncanny knowledge of his own pace. Ideally you should be able to run your race regardless of the rest of the field, secure in the knowledge that in setting yourself that speed you will get your best results.

GENERAL PRINCIPLES OF TRACK TACTICS

(1) Remember that you should always "limber up" (see p. 42) before any event, whether it be 100 Yards, High Jump, or Mile. Just in the same way as a car will go better after the engine has been running for a while, so the muscles function ever so much more efficiently if they are both warm and loosened up. It is therefore of great importance to keep as many clothes on as possible till just before you begin. To my mind a sweater, scarf, and flannel trousers are essential even on a summer's day, so that they are hardly unnecessary in March.

(2) Go "all out" for the first 40 yards or so of *any* race. It will not tire you, but on the contrary will work off that superfluous nervous energy, sometimes called "wind up", and will also get you well into your running, very likely with a useful lead (see p. 75).

(3) As a general rule it is wise to stick to the inside of the track; if you run even a yard wide, you are covering an extra 6 yards or so each lap. At the same time there *is* an exception, which I have dealt with in (5).

(4) The ideal tactics without doubt are those when the runner knows his own pace perfectly, takes the lead at the beginning, and keeps it throughout.

(5) If, however, you have not got the lead, it is a mistake to let your opponents get out of striking distance, which will depend on the length of the race. Perhaps the best plan, if you do not take the lead yourself, is to lie a yard behind the leader. And here is the exception to the rule of keeping to the extreme inside of the track. Under these circumstances I believe it is wiser to run with your inside leg following his outside, for two reasons. If you are right behind him and another man comes up on your outside, you may well be badly "boxed"; whereas if you run slightly wide, you will be in a position to stave off this danger. Also should the leader falter you

can pass him straight away, which would not be possible from the inside position. Examine the photograph of the A.A.A. Half-Mile final in 1928 (Pl. III), which is interesting in this connection.

(6) When you want to pass anyone, do not draw gradually up to him, as this will give him time to respond to your challenge. Make a decisive spurt, using the sprint action for half a dozen strides. If you do this and "shoot" him by a yard or two, it will tend to demoralize your opponent.

(7) Do not make your effort for home too soon, but when you *do* begin, go right through with it. Very few runners can make two sustained efforts successfully in one race, as the strain of accelerating is very tiring. What the length of a finishing effort shall be is an interesting problem. Personally I believe in quality rather than quantity. In other words, a long sprint at the end of a hard race leaves the runner so exhausted in the last 50 yards that he arrives at a walking pace, thereby defeating the whole object of his spurt. Probably the ideal is to quicken up the speed from the $\frac{3}{4}$ distance mark by increasing the vigour of the striding action, but to leave the real sprint to the last 40 or 50 yards. This is of course speaking generally. Details I have left to the next chapter.

(8) Never go into a race thinking "It's no use; I can't possibly do any good". Cultivate confidence and the determination to succeed. The number of comparatively second-rate runners who have beaten tip-toppers because they refused to be frightened by their reputation is very great. Believe me, the "will to win" is worth yards in any race.

Final of Amateur Championship Half Mile, 1928, taken ¾ way round the first lap. The runners are striding easily. Lowe, lying third (×), is just on the outside so as to avoid being boxed and also so that he can break away without delay for his finish. Englehardt, the German (+), his chief rival, is just behind and is running in rhythm with him—a tendency when a runner is watching another. This may be noticed in the rest of the field who tend to run in pairs with the exception of No. 11, who is on the inside and in danger of being boxed.

This is the finish of the above race. Lowe began his finish effort 300 yards from the tape and Englehardt chased him home but failed to pass him.

PLATE III

2   I

4   3

These four photographs were taken of Phil Edwards (the Canadian middle-distance champion) and Douglas Lowe. 1 and 3 are ¾ way round the first lap when both runners are striding; 2 and 4 are 150 yards from the tape. The body carriage, leg and arm action are well worth study.

TRAINING SPEEDS

In books which I have read on athletics such expressions as "jogging", "half and three-quarter speed striding" are frequently used. To my mind these are too vague, as each runner's idea of them differs, often very considerably. In this book much has been made of the necessity of being able to judge speed accurately, and I believe that this can be done right through the training, from the slow "shacking" to the three-quarter speed work. For this reason and in order to avoid any vagueness in this rather important matter, I have made out tables which I hope will be helpful in so far as they should be a standard of comparison.

The principle on which they are based has at least the merit of being simple, though it demands a knowledge of the runner's capacity over his distance at full speed. Having got that or something near it, add roughly one second per hundred yards for three-quarter, two seconds for half, and three seconds for quarter speed. A few examples may be helpful.

Suppose you are entered for several events in the Sports, but the Half-Mile is your strongest distance. Your best performance is about 2 min. 15 sec.—you know that because last year it was won in 2 min. 10 sec. and you were fourth, 20 yards or so back. For training purposes you want to decide your running at three-quarter, half, and quarter speed. In a Half-Mile there are (roughly speaking) nine hundred yards. Adding 1 sec. for each of these, you get for your three-quarter speed 2 min. 15 sec. plus 9 sec. = 2.24. For half speed you add 2 sec. per hundred yards, i.e. 18 sec., making a total of 2.33; and for quarter speed 3 sec. per hundred yards, making 2.42. Now suppose that in the course of your training you want to do three laps of 440 yards each at half speed in order to get stamina. You will try to do each in $\dfrac{2 \cdot 33}{2}$ = 1 min. 16 sec., *i.e.* the three-quarter mile in 3 min. 48 sec. Or perhaps you are aiming at the Quarter-Mile and you can do round about 58 sec.; you want to run 600 yards at three-quarter speed. In a Quarter-Mile there are four hundred yards, so that to find your three-quarter speed you add 4 sec. to your 58, making 62 sec. Here we have a little unitary method.

440 yards are run in 62 sec.

1 yard is run in $\dfrac{62}{440}$ sec.

600 yards are run in $\dfrac{62}{\overset{}{\underset{11}{440}}} \times \overset{15}{600} = \dfrac{930}{11}$.

The answer is 84 sec.

TABLES OF TRAINING SPEEDS

Best Performance over Distance

Top speed	¾ speed	½ speed	¼ speed
100 Yards			
10·5 sec.	11·5	12·5	13·5
11	12	13	14
11·5	12·5	13·5	14·5
12	13	14	15
12·5	13·5	14·5	15·5
13	14	15	16
220 Yards			
30 sec.	32	34	36
28	30	32	34
26	28	30	32
24	26	28	30
23	25	27	29
440 Yards			
54 sec.	58	63	66
56	60	65	68
58	62	67	70
60	64	69	72
65	69	74	79
880 Yards			
2 min. 5 sec.	2.14	2.23	2.32
2 ,, 10 ,,	2.19	2.28	2.37
2 ,, 15 ,,	2.24	2.33	2.42
2 ,, 20 ,,	2.29	2.38	2.47
2 ,, 25 ,,	2.34	2.43	2.52
2 ,, 30 ,,	2.39	2.48	2.57
1 Mile			
4 min. 40 sec.	4.58	5.16	5.34
4 ,, 50 ,,	5.8	5.26	5.44
5 ,, —	5.18	5.36	5.54
5 ,, 10 ,,	5.28	5.46	6.4
5 ,, 20 ,,	5.38	5.56	6.14
5 ,, 30 ,,	5.48	6.6	6.24

CHAPTER V

SOME SUGGESTIONS ABOUT THE SPECIAL PREPARATION AND TRACK TACTICS IN EACH EVENT

I HAVE now dealt with the main principles of training and the technique of running. In this chapter I shall deal as shortly as possible with each of the running events, giving hints on the special preparation necessary for each and also some elementary ideas about the best tactics to employ on the track. It must not be forgotten, however, that the preliminary preparation cannot be omitted, though with boys, who should be naturally pretty fit, it need not be a very prolonged affair. In each event I purpose first to make some general remarks about the race, then give training hints, and finally say something about tactics.

DISTANCES UP TO 100 YARDS

These should be sprinted throughout, and considerable stamina is required to last the distance without serious falling away of speed in the last 30 yards. Few people realize that even the strongest do die away to a certain extent at the end of a Hundred, but the graph in Fig. 25, which shows the time taken over each 10 yards by a very strong runner, is interesting in this connection.

In this race speed, *i.e.* liveliness of action, is all-important, and any fault which causes a loss of time must be severely dealt with, as its results are cumulative, mounting up with each stride. Suppose a clumsy arm action loses even $1/100$ sec. per stride. In 100 yards you perhaps take 50 strides, so that the loss of time over the whole distance will be $1/100 \times 50 = \frac{1}{2}$ sec., which means that you are 4 or 5 yards slower than you would be if the fault were excluded from your action. Looked at in this light, it becomes obvious how necessary it is to make action technique reach as near perfection as possible. Read carefully pages 81–88, in which the sprint action is analysed, especially noting the shortened stride.

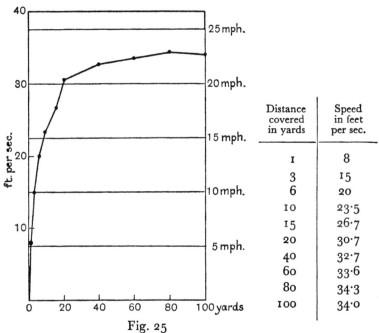

Distance covered in yards	Speed in feet per sec.
1	8
3	15
6	20
10	23·5
15	26·7
20	30·7
40	32·7
60	33·6
80	34·3
100	34·0

Fig. 25

The highest speed was reached between 60 and 80 yards. There is a slight falling off from 80 to 100 even with this runner, who is capable of running 200 yards well inside 20 seconds. The average sprinter, who finds difficulty in lasting the distance at full pressure, has a much greater decrease in speed. Hence the need for stamina.

The two crucial stages in this race are the first 40 and the last 30 yards, for it is at the start and finish that most time can be lost. In other words, the better your starting form and the stronger your finish, the more successful will you be.

TRAINING. Every sprinter should do plenty of three-quarter speed striding over distances from 200 up to 440 yards, for *all* need training in stamina, as the graph given above shows. A certain amount of time should be given up to the knee-lift-striding exercise, for knee-lift is of great importance in sprinting, as it eliminates kick-up and increases leg drive. For speed a very good exercise is as follows. Make two marks on the track about 35 yards apart. Approach the first at an easy half speed stride, but as you pass it break into an all-out sprint, holding it till you reach the second, when you allow yourself to "free wheel" till you come to a standstill. These dashes may be lengthened by 5 yards at a time till you can master 60 or 70 yards, holding your form throughout.

When you are sprinting, never go so fast that you lose your balance or control of your arms. If you do this, you are really travelling slower, not faster, whatever you yourself may feel about it. What it really amounts to is that you must concentrate on style, not speed, for if you think of the first, the second will inevitably follow. Lastly never pull up suddenly at the end of a sprint; it is a short cut to a torn muscle. The start is, of course, a *sine qua non* for the sprinter and it must be practised assiduously. The great difficulty about learning it is that a very considerable strain is imposed on the muscles, so that it is most inadvisable to do more than four fast starts at a stretch (see Chapter VI).

How the training time is arranged will depend largely on the type of runner. Roughly speaking, if speed is needed, starting-practice, plus plenty of *short* dashes as above, will be needed; but when I say "plenty" I mean never more than half-a-dozen at an outside maximum. Try to get your legs and arms to work together at their highest possible speed and keep your stride "clipped".

If stamina is wanting, *i.e.* there is a lack of finish, do plenty of three-quarter speed striding, as suggested above, quickening up to a sprint finish over the last 20 or 30 yards. Not more than two of these stamina exercises should be undertaken in an afternoon. Make out some kind of training programme for yourself based on these principles. Conditions and individual differences are so great that it is almost impossible to make out a time-table which would be of much use, besides which half the fun of athletics is lost if one does not work out one's own salvation.

TACTICS. As the race is sprinted and there are no bends, track tactics in the ordinary sense of the word do not enter into the question. There are, however, certain things which the experienced sprinter will always do. (1) Never run in a race till you have "limbered up". In other words, always do some stretching exercises— toe touching and high kicking are two of the best—and run a furlong, working up very gradually to an "all out" burst of 30 yards or so. You will do all the better for it and considerably diminish the risk of tearing a muscle, which is the especial bugbear of the sprinter. (2) Do all you can to rest your legs and keep them warm till you actually strip for the race. Wear some trousers over your shorts and do not walk about on your toes, as it tends to tighten up the muscles of the calves. (3) When your turn comes to run, keep calm and concentrate hard on the matter in hand—to run your best without thinking of anyone else. (4) Fix your eyes on some mark 20 yards beyond the finish and run right through the tape. Above all, *do not* look round or throw up your arms. If you can manage to dip forward from the waist just as you reach the tape, well and good; otherwise your best plan by far is to go right through the tape as though it were not there. (5) Do not worry about the ability of the other runners. More races have been lost by suggestion of defeat than you would believe.

200 AND 220 YARDS

These races are generally called sprints, but, strictly speaking, the term is incorrect as applied to them. Very few men indeed can carry through a whole furlong with the sprinting action. I would go as far as to say that anyone, however strong he may be, will gain by using a striding action in the middle stage of these races.

TRAINING. The preparation is much the same as for the shorter race, except that every one *must* do the striding work at quarter and half speed over distances of 300 up to 440 yards. The speed-work is the same, but an exercise should be added to develop the power of changing from the striding to the sprinting action. Alternate 100-yards quarter speed striding with 50-yards sprints, starting with 200 and working up to 400 yards.

TACTICS. Sometimes this race is run round bends without a separate lane for each runner, or a start in echelon. This is generally fatal to runners on the outside, as they must either go much further than the inside man or else drop behind the field, thereby being shut out for the rest of the race. Under these circumstances the only thing to do, if you are on the outside, is to make up your mind to be the first to reach the corner in order to get the inside berth; but remember that you must have a lead of 2 yards before you can cut in on another runner. Fortunately this type of race is now the exception rather than the rule and it is generally run in lanes. The tactics are then resolved into a question of pace-judgment.

The best way to run the race is to go the first 50 yards "all out", then break into a full-speed stride action, leaving your final spurt for the last 50 yards or so. You should, of course, experiment yourself and see how you feel. There is no doubt, however, that it is a mistake to sprint over the whole distance, as even the strongest man when doing so tires to such an extent that he loses more in the last 50 than he gains in the first 170 yards. Moreover, the stride action gets you over the ground wonderfully quickly, as I have found to my surprise many times.

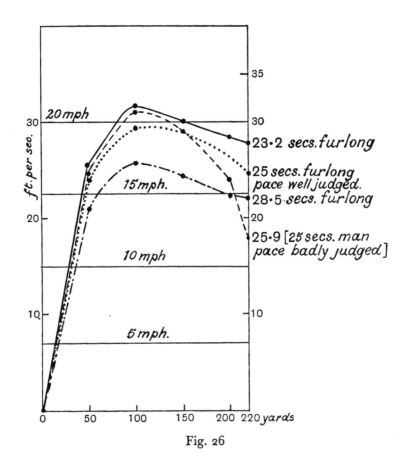

Fig. 26

Table of the times at the intermediate stages, in seconds

These times will not of course necessarily apply to all runners. They are based on the following assumptions. The first stage of 50 is the slowest, when speed is being picked up. The second stage between 50 and 100 is the fastest. Thereafter there is a decline in speed till the finish as the runner tires. On the graph is plotted the speed in feet per second of the 23-second, the 25-second, the 28.5-second running and also that of a runner who could, *if he had judged his pace correctly*, have done 25 sec. As it was,

50	100	150	200	220
7·0	12·6	18·6	25·4	28
6·8	12·2	18·0	24·4	27
6·6	11·8	17·4	23·5	26
6·3	11·4	16·8	22·6	25
6·1	11·0	16·2	21·8	24
5·7	10·6	15·4	20·8	23

his speed fell off badly at the end of the race because he had made the pace too hot for himself over the first 100 yards. Note the quick decline in speed as compared with the other three, whose performances were better balanced, *i.e.* they left enough energy for their final effort.

440 YARDS

The Americans call this race a "dash", but it must be emphasized again, as in the case of the Furlong, that there can be no question of sprinting the whole distance. The same sort of speed tactics are appropriate as for the Furlong, except that the striding should be for the Furlong runner somewhere between half and three-quarter, not full speed (see Table on p. 67).

TRAINING. For the sprinter this is a hard race, needing plenty of stamina-training if he is to last the course. Quarter-speed striding (see Table on p. 67) over 880 and 600 yards is to my mind essential for every quarter-miler. Personally, when training for this distance I make a point of doing a 600 yards each week as fast as I can comfortably manage without putting in a finish. This work over the longer distance not only gives the necessary staying power, but also has a psychological effect, as it gives confidence for the shorter distance; many runners, however, tend to shirk it because of its strenuousness.

Speed, of course, must not be neglected, and indeed it should be the middle-distance runner's main objective. For this purpose the scheme suggested for the 100 and 220 yards should be ideal, but over rather longer distances. Besides this, try to find out what is your best speed for the middle stage of the race and practise running at that speed over a 100 yards with a flying start; this is useful for developing pace-judgment. Finally, do not neglect the start, as it often is of first-rate importance to get a lead in the first 50 yards, so that you can take the inside berth at the first corner.

TACTICS. Nowadays on the continent and in America this race is run in lanes, and in consequence everything depends on pace-judgment. In England, however, this is as yet not so, and in many ways it adds to the interest, though not perhaps from the point of view of the man in the outside position.

The race generally starts with a rush for the inside of the track at the first corner, and lucky the man who gets it. The ideal way of running the race is to get the lead and keep it—a full-speed burst at the start, and having gained impetus drop into an easy, bounding stride action

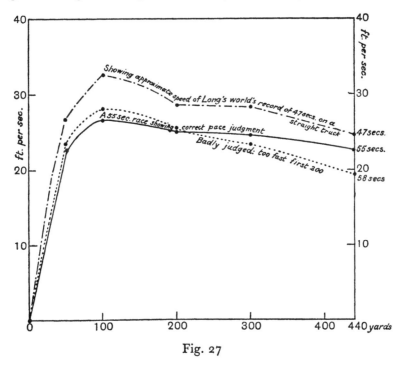

Fig. 27

On the graph the top curve shows Long's record of 47 sec. on a straight track. The others show a 55-sec. man running his race correctly and in the dotted curve making the pace too hot for himself in the first half of the distance, thereby adding three seconds to his time through failing in the last 100 yards.

with the weight forward on the balls of the feet; finally a spurt carefully timed to take you through the tape feeling that you still have a little reserve strength left if need had arisen. This, I say, is the *ideal* way, because you are independent of the other runners and can set the pace to suit yourself. At the same time it requires a lot of confidence in your own pace-judgment, and most novices prefer to let others do the pace-making.

If, then, you cannot, or would not, get the lead, the next best thing is to hang on to the man who has, running a few inches wide of him. There are two reasons for this. In the first place there is much less risk of your being boxed if another runner comes up on your outside. Secondly you are in a better position to "shoot" the leader directly he shows signs of faltering. The extra yard or two covered in a lap seem to me worth it.

Remember, however, that in your training you should aim always at learning to run your own race by knowing your own pace within a fifth of a second over the intermediate stages. Study the table and make up your mind what your best pace will be.

Table of Times at the Intermediate Stages

50	100	200	300	440
6·3	11·9	23·4	35·0	53·0
6·6	12·2	24·1	36·3	55·0
6·8	12·8	25·4	37·8	57·0
7·0	13·2	26·2	39·0	59·0
7·4	13·5	27·0	41·4	61·0

The Table assumes a full-speed crouch start and use of the sprint action up to 50 yards. Thereafter the runner strides through up to 40 or 50 yards from the tape, when he breaks into the sprint action for his finishing burst.

880 YARDS

Strength without style becomes more and more at a discount the longer the race. The striding action, speed without effort, is the keynote of successful half-miling, plus—and it is a big item—a carefully developed finishing sprint. The first-rate half-miler will, of course, suit his tactics to the contingencies of the race; but if he can, he will make his finishing effort at a certain distance from the tape, knowing that so he can get the best out of himself.

TRAINING. For stamina, quarter-speed striding (see Table, p. 67) over 1000 yards up to a mile is essential for those who find difficulty in lasting the distance. Those who are primarily long-distance runners can best develop speed by taking the class above their own in the table on p. 67 and run at that speed over distances from 300 to 600 yards. All should practise changing from the stride to the sprint action by adapting the exercise suggested on p. 72 for the Furlong.

The sprint finish is also of very great importance. Probably it can best be learnt by running a lap (440 yards) aiming to do the time as for the first lap of the race; then, having completed the lap, put in a finish of 25 or 30 yards, which may be lengthened by 5 yards at a time till you can master whatever you find best for yourself. In my opinion very few boys, if they have run their race at the right speed, *i.e.* not too slowly, can with advantage manage a finish of much over 60 yards.

1st lap	2nd lap	Time
		m. s.
63	62	2 5
66	64	2 10
69	66	2 15
71	69	2 20
73	72	2 25
76	74	2 30

It will be seen that the first lap is slightly slower than the second. Generally this is best for immature runners. The ability to stand a fast first quarter-mile will come later. It is urged that great care should be taken in deciding the best time for the first half of the race, for by setting too fast a pace here, even by one second, as much as three or four may well be added on the time for the whole distance.

TACTICS. As in the case of the Quarter-Mile, there is a great deal to be said for taking the lead and keeping it. In any case you should learn by experience the time which suits you best for the first lap, experimenting with times between two seconds faster and two seconds slower than the time given in the table. Albert Hill, who won the 800 and 1500 metres at the Olympic Games in 1920, knew within $\frac{1}{5}$th second what he was doing at each lap.

That is what you should aim to be able to do. Learn pace-judgment, cultivate your finish and the ability to change into the sprint action for purposes of passing an opponent, and you will not go far wrong. If you must be behind, try always to be within striking distance of the leaders, *i.e.* 3 or 4 yards, and never forget that if you feel tired the others are probably just as bad, so "keep your pecker up".

MILE

The Mile differs from the Half-Mile chiefly in the need for more stamina, or, shall I say, greater economy of effort. Hence easy striding at an even pace throughout the race is the ideal. As has been said before, the greater the distance, the less knee-lift should be used. This, however, does not mean that knee-lift exercises should be omitted from the training, but that knee-lift used in the race must be absolutely natural, *i.e.* a matter of habit and not of conscious effort.

Pace-judgment again is of the greatest importance. The time-table given below should be carefully studied. Notice that the first lap is generally the fastest owing to the sprint start; the middle two are the slowest, when the runner is holding on to a pace well within his powers, so that he can quicken up and put in a finishing spurt in the last lap.

TRAINING. The half-miler who wants to train-on for the Mile should do some slow striding at quarter and half speed (see Table, p. 67) over 1¼ to 1½ miles, also some hip swinging and knee-lift exercises from 50 yards to a furlong, or perhaps it would be safer to say "as far as possible without over-strain". Generally, however, at school it is the cross-country men who go for the Mile as their chief track event, and their concern is mainly to get the necessary speed. For this purpose any of the sprinting exercises will help to liven up the action and develop the power of

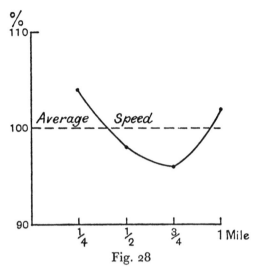

Fig. 28

This graph shows percentage deviation from the average speed over the whole distance for each lap when the pace-judgment is good. Hill's record conforms almost exactly to these figures, while George and Nurmi are a trifle more regular in their running.

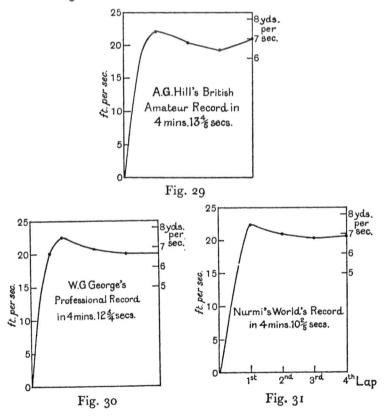

A.G.Hill's British Amateur Record in 4 mins.13⅘ secs.

Fig. 29

W.G George's Professional Record in 4 mins.12¾ secs.

Fig. 30

Nurmi's World's Record in 4 mins.10⅖ secs.

Fig. 31

sprinting which is of such importance to milers. Now and again it is a wise plan to put in a good striding 440 or 600 yards at the speed of the class one above your own in the table, in order to vary the monotony.

TACTICS. In this race again, as in the others, the leader has a great advantage. Nothing is more disturbing than running in a crowd when your natural stride is being chopped and the risk of being "boxed" or elbowed is considerable. The first 50 yards, then, should be run as a sprint, after which an even pace should be maintained throughout until the finishing spurt is begun. Perhaps, however, it is more accurate to say that you should drop into an easy stride well within your powers and try to keep the rhythm of your action as even as possible. As a matter of fact, your speed is bound to fall off slightly in the third lap, which is always the most trying. But, as the song says, "rhythm is the thing", so that if you want to get the best out of yourself, find out what stride suits you and hold on to it for all you are worth. If you cannot get the lead, hang on to the leaders and beware of being "boxed". Read the section on the Quarter and Half-Mile, as much of the advice about tactics, though not about speed, holds good for the Mile.

Table of times at the intermediate stages

Quarter mile	Half mile	Three-quarter mile	1 mile
	m. s.	m. s.	m. s.
66·5	2 18	3 31	4 40
69·5	2 22	3 37·5	4 50
72·0	2 28·5	3 46·5	5 0
74·5	2 33	3 53·2	5 10
77·0	2 38	4 1·5	5 20
79·0	2 43·5	4 9·5	5 30
81·5	2 48	4 16·6	5 40

In each of these Miles the first lap is the fastest, helped by the fast start; the last is the next fastest, when the runner is putting in his finish. The third is the slowest, and it is this stage of the race which has always to be watched by all milers, but especially so by those who incline to lack stamina.

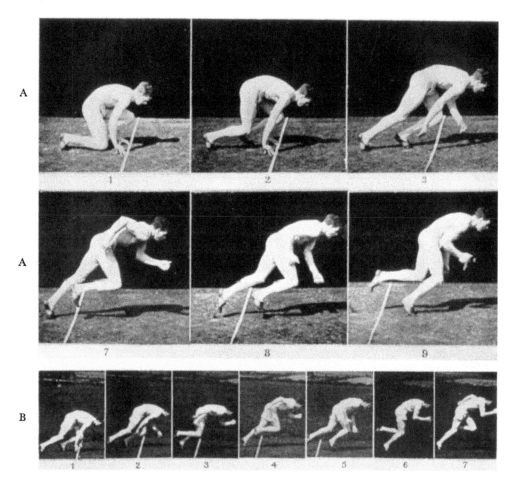

THE CROUCH START

A. *"Out of the holes."* Notes. (1) Perfectly relaxed position. (2) Body tensed and weight thrown forward on to hands and left leg. Eyes fixed on spot where first stride will come. 3–6 show the falling forward tendency of the body which is counterbalanced by the upper cut of the left hand (see 6). The arm action lacks vigour. If the drive from the left hand had been really powerful the right arm would—and should—have swung further to the rear than it has done in 6. Actually it ought to be more flexed to keep it in control, as well as further back. 7–9 show the short first stride, in this case about 1 ft. 6 in. The left arm should be more flexed, especially in 9. 10 shows an over upright position caused by the push from the right leg. This could have been righted by a forward dip from the waist, as in 11 and 12. In 12 the arm action is good except for the left hand which has been flung too far behind the body and is thus momentarily out of control. The remedy would have been a greater flex at the elbow. The angle is fairly good though the forward lean might have been more pronounced with advantage. 3, 4 and 5 show a straight line effect in the right arm. This can hardly fail to have slowed up its backward swing.

PLATE V

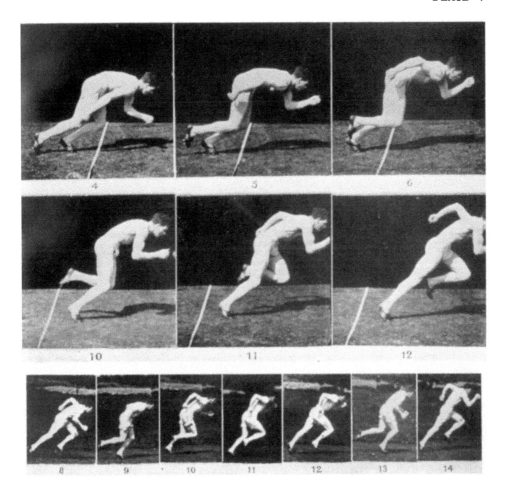

B. *Getting into the running. Notes.* This series shows the gradual raising of the body to the normal sprinting angle. The chief faults are, as in Series A, an insufficient arm action in the first two strides; the arms not enough flexed at the elbow thereby causing a more clumsy and less lively action (see 2, 3, 4, 5, 9 and 13), and also, especially in 11 and 13, the body being pushed up into an erect position by the downward drive of the foot. This calls for a dip at the waist as suggested above. Notice that the foreleg is not stretched out for a full stride but is clipped in so that the body is well over it as it lands (see 6, 9, 13) and as little time as possible is wasted in the air.

CHAPTER VI

THE CROUCH START

In the old days the professional sprinters used a "stand up" start, which was probably as quick as any modern "crouch" start. The "dab" start, as used by them, is practically a lost art now, and in any case takes so much learning that it is not worth while for the ordinary amateur to tackle it. I do not, of course, mean to suggest that the "crouch" start is easy, but if you go the right way about it, it is not at all impossible to become quite moderately proficient in a comparatively short time.

In my experience, boys who have learnt to do the "crouch" start *well* gain two to four yards over the "any-old-how-stand-up-brigade". But the latter gains at least two yards over those who try to do the "crouch" and do it all wrong. The moral is: do not use the "crouch" in a race till you have had some practice; it simply does not pay.

THE POSITION. The first thing is to get the initial position right, and this is most important, as, should it be faulty, your speed will be seriously affected. Which foot you put behind does not matter, so long as it is always the same one. With most people it is the stronger, and for purposes of detail I am assuming that it is the right foot. A quick and easy method of taking up your position is as follows. Stand with the toes of both feet just touching the line. Drop the left foot back till the toes are on a level with the heel of your right foot. You then have the position of the hole for your front foot. Next kneel down with your right knee resting against the heel of your left foot. The toes of your right foot should be in the correct position for the back hole (see Pl. V, A 1). Before you actually dig the holes, look along your lane towards the tape and make quite certain that you are perfectly square. The positions of the above holes may of course need modification to suit individuals. The short, stockily built man can bring both holes an inch or so closer together and nearer the line, while the tall, leggy type may need more spread.

Now, having got your feet correctly placed, you can dig your holes. The depth of these should be just sufficient to support the balls of the feet. The back wall of each should be absolutely perpendicular, as this gives better foothold than the sloping surface. The front of the holes, however, should slope forwards and allow the feet to come out unhindered.

"Get to your Marks!" So much, then, for the feet. When the starter gives the command "Get to your marks!" the preliminary position is taken up. Very little, however, need be said about this, as the photo (Pl. V, A 1) speaks for itself. Note that at this point you should try to keep as relaxed as possible; it is only when the command "Get set!" is given that the body is tensed.

"Get Set!" (see Pl. V, A 2). The absolute essential of this second position is that the weight must go right forward on to the hands and the left leg, chiefly the former. If you do not do this you are bound to lose at least two yards on those who do. How far the hands should be apart is a matter for personal decision, but they should not be more than six or less than three inches wide of the lines on which the legs move as they come out of the holes. If they are too wide your body will tend to nose-dive into the ground, and if too close you have not a wide enough base to take the weight of your body. All one can say is that you should feel comfortable and balanced.

There are two types of hand-rest, of which I personally favour *A* (Fig. 32), though I used *B* (Fig. 33) for many years. *A* seems to me preferable because it gives a firmer and higher support. Those who favour *B* say that it gets you further forward, but I question whether this is an advantage, for the same reason that an over-wide hand-spread seems to be a mistake. Some sprinters, again, believe in bending the arms, but personally I think they should be kept straight, so as to raise the shoulders as far from the ground as possible.

When the command "Get set" is given, then you transfer the weight of your body forward on to your hands and left leg. Do this smoothly and not too suddenly, or you will tend to overbalance. The starter, if he knows

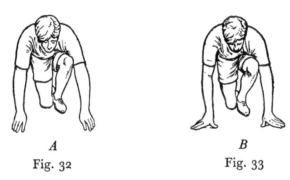

A	B
Fig. 32	Fig. 33

his business, will give you plenty of time and make quite certain that you are steady before he "fires you off."

Study the position in Pl. V, A 2 carefully. Notice that the right knee is raised from the ground in such a way that there is a slight slope from the knee down to the ankle (this leg is quite loose and has no weight on it at all). Ideally the back should be straight and parallel with the ground, but this depends on the build of the runner and in some cases cannot be achieved. The eyes are fixed on the point where the first stride will come. Some runners raise their heads and keep their eyes on the mark. But this seems to me to put a heavy strain on the neck muscles besides tending to cause a prematurely upright position.

You should experiment for yourself with various foot

and hand positions till you find what suits you best. Remember that it is essential to be absolutely poised and steady in your "set" position, so that you are capable of staying there as firm as a rock as long as the starter cares to keep you waiting (some delay as long as 4 or 5 seconds, though generally it will not be more than 2 or 3).

ACTION OUT OF THE HOLES. There are two departments in the art of starting, first the actual quickness off the mark, and secondly speed of acceleration in "getting into your running". Of these the latter is considerably the more important, and it is the commonest fault to sacrifice speed over the first 50 yards for a jump out of the holes.

The first idea to get rid of is that the "crouch" start is like the spring of a cat. For the vast majority of sprinters there should be no question of a jump out of the holes, but rather there should be a steady rush forwards—an even acceleration to top speed in the shortest possible time compatible with holding sprinting form.

The most common fault in starting is getting the body upright too soon, which is largely a matter of stride-lengths. If you spring out of the holes or take too long a first stride, you will almost inevitably get up into an erect position immediately. Actually the body should gradually assume the correct sprinting angle, and this should take from 5 to 10 strides. The smaller the man and the neater his footwork, the quicker will he be into his running; but for the heavy-weight who is also long in the leg this problem is always difficult. The length of the first stride should vary between 9 and 18 inches in front of the line. This is not really an effort to gain ground, but rather the initial movement for getting you smoothly into your running. In other words, the drive out of the holes does not come from the back foot but from the front. The second and subsequent strides must combine speed with power. An over-long stride will cause a sacrifice of forward lean, and the strides should lengthen regularly till the normal sprinting angle be attained.

Fig. 34 shows two practice starts of mine in 1927. It will be noticed how much more regular the second attempt was than the first; this is probably due to the fact that the muscles were more flexible after their efforts in the first run. Maximum striding was reached in just over 30 yards at the seventeenth stride, and be it

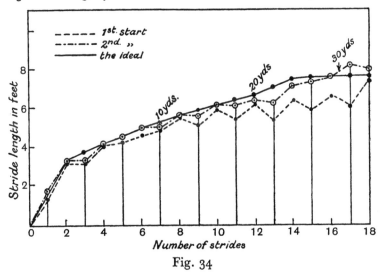

Fig. 34

noted that it was 8 ft., which is too long for a sprinter, who, in my opinion, should never exceed 7 ft. 6 in. at an outside maximum. These measurements were taken on a grass track, and in order to get the prints of the feet I anointed my shoes with white. The plain line on the graph is the goal at which I was aiming, *i.e.* a steady increase of stride-length up to $7\frac{1}{2}$ feet in the first 25 yards and absolute regularity of striding for the rest of the distance.

Having dealt with the legs, we now come to the arm action, which, without exaggeration, is quite as important, if not more so. If you want to test this statement, try making a dash from a standing position first without and then with the help of your arms; the difference will be fairly apparent. In teaching anyone the "crouch" start I should always advise him to concentrate on his arm action. If the arms are working correctly, the chances are that the legs are also, for they are largely controlled by the arms.

In the "Set" position the weight of the body, as has been said before, is right forward on to the hands and front foot. As the pistol fires, the left arm flies forward in a vicious upper-cut with the elbow well flexed. It is on this movement of the left arm, which comes forward with the right leg, that the runner should concentrate. At a moment such as this, entailing considerable nervous strain, it is no good trying to think of two things at once. Aim to bring that arm into action as the striker of the pistol hits the cap but before it fires the cartridge. If you do that it will give you the necessary mental alertness and will help to cut out that momentary paralysis which seizes so many sprinters when they hear the report of the starting pistol.

The first few strides demand an arm action of upper cuts, *i.e.* with the emphasis on the upward and forward swing. This is essential in order to pick up the equilibrium of the body, as its immediate tendency is to pitch forward when the arms start work, thereby removing two of its props. After these few strides the arms will quite naturally drop into the true sprint action, with the emphasis on the downward and backward pull.

The two most common faults are those of swinging the arms diagonally across the body, which inclines to upset the runner's balance, and of failing to keep the arms flexed. If the movements are going to be really lively it is obvious that the swing of the arms must be a short one. Hence the need for a flexed elbow; otherwise the straight arm cannot but be too sluggish for movements of which the essence is speed.

In order to attain the gradual raising of the body to the requisite sprinting angle, three things will be necessary: a gradual lengthening of stride; a vigorous execution of the arm action detailed above, and also a bend forward

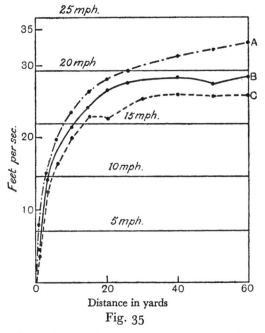

Fig. 35

Graph to show the acceleration in ft. per sec. of three runners: *A*, the champion; *B*, the average; and *C*, the novice. Note especially the smoothness of *A*'s running as contrasted with *B* and *C*. *B* faltered between 45 and 55 yards, while *C*'s striding is very erratic from 15 to 30.

These results were obtained by means of electrical timing. Incidentally *A*'s start was a very fine one. The figures are reproduced by kind permission from *Living Machinery* by Prof. A. V. Hill. (G. Bell and Sons.)

at the waist for the first half-dozen strides. This is necessary in order to off-set the violence of the leg action which is tending to raise the body into an upright position after the first falling forward tendency has been counterbalanced.

No one who has tried to do this kind of start will pretend that it is easy. Perhaps the greatest difficulty in learning it is due to the fact that it is not possible to practice many at a time, three or four "all out" efforts being quite sufficient, owing to the muscular strain involved. The best way to get the action correctly is to practice the motions as slowly as you can, concentrating entirely on style. Even so, half a dozen starts will be plenty. These slow starts are absolutely essential at the beginning of each season, even for the tried performer. The mechanism of the action has got to be so much a part of you that you cannot help doing it correctly. Certainly you will not be able to bother about correct style when you are starting in a race, and almost inevitably you will find difficulty with your body-lean in the first 25 or 30 yards. If possible, it is most advisable to get a friend to watch your practice-starts to see whether you are raising your body too soon. Do not let him stand too near, otherwise he will not be able to get a perspective view; 20 or 30 yards is about the right distance. A camera is also a useful critic; I have dealt with this in the section "Photography in Athletics" in Appendix C, p. 143.

CHAPTER VII

HURDLING

PERHAPS if a number of athletes were asked in which
event they would rather excel, over half would decide
on hurdling. And indeed there is a great deal to be said
for it. From the competitor's point of view it is amazingly
good fun flying hurdles, when it is done well, whether
racing or only in practice. It does not leave a man more
dead than alive, like some barbarous races. Nor is there,
to any great extent, the sprinter's danger of snapped
muscles. Lastly it needs less natural talent than other
events and repays trouble at an extraordinarily high
percentage, as I shall try to show.

The race consists of ten flights of hurdles, 3 ft. 6 in.
high, at intervals of 10 yards with 15 yards at each end.
For boys under sixteen it is strongly advisable to make
the hurdles 3 ft. high with intervals of 9 yards. Even
seniors will benefit by having them at 3 ft. 4 in. instead
of the regulation 3½ ft., though in their case the 10-yard
intervals may be kept. It is of the utmost importance
that boys should learn to take the hurdles in good style
without straining themselves, as they are bound to do if
they attempt to tackle full-size hurdles with the regulation intervals. Also in order to breed confidence it is
much best either to use a light hurdle, or preferably one
with a heavy frame and a detachable top which falls off
when it is hit. Fig. 1 on p. 18 shows a plan of a hurdle
which after a season's trial has proved itself to be very
suitable for boys.

PHYSICAL QUALIFICATIONS. (1) *Height.* The greatest
hurdlers have almost all been in the neighbourhood of
6 ft., and the tall man has a big pull over a short one in
that he can stride over the hurdles, whereas the smaller

must perforce jump them—anyway, it is an event which demands length of leg.

(2) *Suppleness.* This is an absolute necessity, and especially must the hip joint be unbelievably flexible. The only way to attain this is by means of various stretching exercises, which will be given in detail later. Any boy of sixteen or under should be capable of doing these, though it may come only gradually and at first be a painful business. A very muscular man will rarely be a great stylist, though he may become a useful performer through sheer pace and strength. It is the long-limbed, supple fellow who is best endowed physically to be a great hurdler, and without exaggeration it may be said that if such a one is keen enough and can find someone to help him with his training there is no reason why he should not become first-rate.

One thing there is which is by no means necessary and may even prove a handicap. A man need not be able to run fast to become a good hurdler. Many of the greatest performers in the world have been comparatively slow over a hundred yards. I have in mind also a boy, once almost laughably sluggish as a runner, who can now do something inside $17\frac{1}{2}$ seconds over hurdles and will do better still before he leaves school. Neither is he the exception, but rather the rule. I have been amazed at the way hurdlers have improved their speed, and it seems to me that a course of hurdling is one of the best ways of improving a man's sprinting ability.

THE NEED FOR STYLE. In almost every other event the natural athlete with a fine turn of speed, great strength, or exceptional spring may become a really useful performer even though lacking in style. This I believe to be an impossibility in the 120 Yards Hurdles. Style is three-quarters of the battle. It will be as well, then, to understand just what style will do for a hurdler. Really it consists in just this: the ability to *stride* over the hurdles, spending as short a time in the air and losing as little momentum at each clearance as possible.

In order to realize more vividly the need for style, let us embark on a few simple mathematical calculations. There are in all ten hurdles to be cleared. The enthusiastic beginner jumps them all with enormous vigour. At each hurdle he not only spends a most unnecessarily long time suspended in space, but each time he lands both legs come to earth simultaneously and his body is jerked into an upright position. Thereby he loses time both in clearing the hurdle and also in picking up his running again. The expert, who can actually run the same pace on the flat as the beginner, seems to "snap" over the hurdle, taking it smoothly in his stride, and may well gain as much as half a second over each clearance if his style is first-rate. Multiply this by ten, *i.e.* the number of flights, and you will observe that the expert gains 5 seconds over the full flight. Thus his time will be, shall we say, 15 seconds, while the novice's will be 20 seconds; yet they both run their 120 yards flat race in $12\frac{1}{2}$ seconds.

There is not room in this book to discuss the respective merits of the old bent leg as compared with the more modern straight leg style of hurdling—the latter is so immeasurably superior, as may be seen by comparing the performances in the Amateur Championships of fifty years ago with those of to-day. In those days the winning times were round about 17 seconds; now they are generally 15 seconds or under, if the conditions are favourable.

THE STRAIGHT LEG STYLE ANALYSED. The main principle to be kept in mind is that every part of the body is brought into play to achieve a lightning clearance from take-off to landing and the least possible loss of time in taking up the running after landing. In order to get this clear, it will be best to take each limb separately and see how it functions.

(a) *The leading (left) leg.* This may be either left or right, though generally the stronger should be kept for the rear, and in this description the left leg will lead. At the take-off this is flicked up straight to the front so that the heel just clears the top of the hurdle. Great care should be taken to resist the tendency to swing sideways, as many hurdlers are inclined to do. It means a certain lack of balance which must be compensated by a definite mus-cular effort, with loss of both time and energy. Notice also that the expression was "flicked up", not "gently raised". There must be real power and snap in the upward move-ment, though later the tall hurdler may be able to modify the stiff-leg swing into something rather like the action of a high-trotting horse. Gaby has to a certain extent done this, as may be seen in the photos on Pls. VI and VII ; but the beginner is strongly advised against it. This leg should come to the ground just as quickly and as close to the hurdle as possible. A first-class hurdler going at full speed takes off 6 or 7 feet from the hurdle and lands $3\frac{1}{2}$ to $4\frac{1}{2}$ feet the other side of it. The faster you run, the further away you take off and the further from the hurdle you tend to land. It is hard to lay down definite distances, which must depend on the size of the hurdle, the height of the hurdler, and the speed of the approach. A boy should never take off much nearer than $4\frac{1}{2}$ feet or further than $6\frac{1}{2}$ feet from the hurdle. He should aim to land as near it as possible, *i.e.* anything from 3 to $4\frac{1}{2}$ feet. In practice it is useful to put down a piece of paper—say 3 ft. on the further side of the hurdle, and try to hit it with your leading left leg as you land. At the same time, although the foot should be snapped downwards, it is a mistake to over-emphasize this movement, as it may well lead to loss of balance. Really the rear (right) leg will be doing the work at this stage of the clearance, as will be shown.

(b) *The rear (right) leg* should be mainly passive during

HURDLING

Notice the action of the right arm, stretching forwards and downwards towards the top of the hurdle, bringing the body right forward with it. After the hurdle is passed, it is kept close to the body and slightly flexed so that it may be in perfect control and ready to punch through for the normal running arm action. The action of the rear leg is delayed. After taking off it trails inactively, till the leading leg reaches the top of the hurdle (5). It then swings through with a sideways movement at right angles to the body. Having cleared the cross-bar by a narrow margin, immediately the foot is clear (10) it travels upward and forward for a big knee lift, so that the first stride after the clearance may be a full one. Note especially the positions from 11–15.

PLATE VI

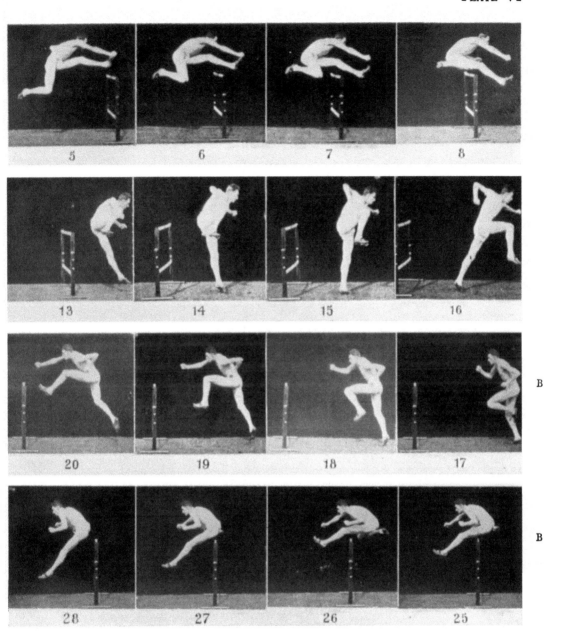

B

B

In 17–32 the leading leg (left) and rear arm (left) may be clearly followed. The left leg is flicked up so that the heel just misses the crossbar (22) and is chopped down as close as possible on the further side of the hurdle. The left arm is flexed and kept well into the side during the first part of the clearance (17–26), so that it may be in position to come forward with the rear leg (27–32) and maintain the body in a straightforward position. The great majority of hurdlers lose control of this arm which flies out sideways and thereby slows up the action (see Pl. XIV, A).

the first half of the clearance after it has given the impetus for the stride. That is to say, it should be trailed behind until the leading (left) leg has just cleared the top of the hurdle and is beginning to descend.

At this moment the rear (right) leg becomes extremely active. It swings up and round in such a way that the thigh is parallel with the top of the hurdle, and the knee, which is bent, clears it by an inch or so. This swing-through of the rear leg is perhaps the most important movement to do correctly in the whole action—and the most difficult, as the hip joint needs to be tremendously supple for the position to be held. From the beginner's point of view, the trouble is to swing the knee through

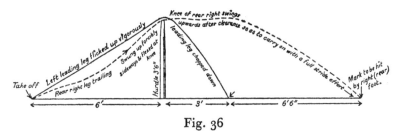

Fig. 36

high enough without dropping the toe and catching the top of the hurdle *en passant*. At first he will probably be unable to swing the knee high enough; in which case he will either hit the hurdle with it or he will fly too high in order to avoid doing so.

When the rear leg has cleared the hurdle, there will be a strong temptation to drop it prematurely in order to get the foot to the ground as quickly as possible. This is wrong, as it shortens the next stride and will make it difficult to reach the next hurdle in the regulation three strides. You should aim to swing the knee up as high as possible on its way forward into its next stride, and in this respect you cannot do better than copy Gaby, though Earl Thompson, the present World's Record holder, also gets the same tremendous knee-lift.

In order to develop this full stride with the rear (right) leg as it swings through after clearing the hurdle, you should find out what your natural running stride is. Suppose this is 6 ft. Put down one piece of paper 3 ft. beyond the hurdle to be hit by your leading (left) leg, and 6 ft. 6 in. further on, *i.e.* a little over your usual stride effort, another piece of paper which you will aim to hit with rear (right) foot.

The swing-through of the rear (right) leg, which should be really snappy and powerful, automatically hastens the descent of the leading (left) foot to the ground.

(c) *The leading (right) arm.* Even more perhaps than in sprinting, the arm action is of the utmost importance. As the leading (left) leg rises towards the hurdle, the leading (right) arm is stretched vigorously forward and downwards, towards the top of the hurdle. This controls the body and keeps it well forward.

(d) *The rear (left) arm.* The management of this is perhaps the greatest difficulty that most hurdlers have to tackle, whether they be beginners or champions. The tendency of this wayward limb is to get out of control as the body clears the hurdle (see Pl. XIV, A, p. 143). It flies out like a wing, sideways and upwards, thereby losing that precious fraction of a second before it can be punched through for the next stride in harmony with the rear (right) leg, as it should be. Ideally it should be kept flexed at the elbow, with the hand lightly clenched, close to the hip and never far behind it. In this way it is ready to carry on the good work immediately on landing without pause. Gaby has perfected this; and you cannot do better than study the photographs in Pl. VI, 17–32, p. 92, where the action of his rear (left) arm can clearly be seen. Here it may be said that commonly even among the best performers the rear arm is rather a hindrance than a help.

To summarize: the arms should as far as possible be kept well into the sides and, except in the case of the leading arm at the beginning of the clearance, should be flexed as in sprinting; they are much more easily controlled thus. The tendency to fly out sideways will be found very strong and may be best counteracted by aiming to swing a little inward instead of straight backward and forward.

(e) *The body.* This should always maintain a forward lean. On landing it is most important that the sprinting body-angle should be held. The ability to maintain this will depend on the arms and stomach muscles. The latter will have to take considerable strain in holding the body forward regardless of the violent action of the legs; but the arms, if used correctly, will help very much.

If you study the photographs on Pl. VI, 1–32, p. 92, and Pl. VII, 46–60, p. 96, and concentrate on the body-angle, you will find that at the beginning of the clearance the leading (right) arm is reaching straight forward and rather downward, so that at one moment the chin almost touches the leading (left) knee, thereby taking the body with it. In practice every movement should be exaggerated, especially this body-dip in rising to the hurdle. After the top of the hurdle has been passed you will notice that the extreme body-dip gradually gives place to the normal sprinting angle. At the same time most people find it so difficult not to land in an upright position that an extra body-dip from the waist at the moment of descent is strongly to be recommended. Indeed, the man who can hold a "falling" angle towards the end of a hard-fought race has a tremendous asset, and this has probably gone far towards winning Gaby his Championships during the past two years, if it be possible to pick out any one point in an almost perfect style.

Apart from the forward lean it is of great importance that, throughout the clearance, the shoulders should be kept square to the front and that there should be no sideway lean from the waist towards the rear leg, as passes the top of the hurdle. If he does this the hurdler tends to land sideways and loses time in regaining his balance. The cause is a lack of flexibility in the hip and the remedy an increase of exercises to obtain it.

TRAINING. Training may be split up into two parts: stamina and general fitness on the one hand, and the attainment of perfect technique on the other. For the question of fitness it will be best to turn to Chapter III. At the same time it may be well to detail here three things on which you should concentrate. (1) The *start*, of which a full description is given in Chapter VI. Do not neglect this, as a poor approach to the first hurdle may well throw you out of your stride for the rest of the race; also it is extremely hard to hold your form when the rest of the field are two yards ahead of you. The result is the same as when you are playing golf with a man who drives a much longer ball than yourself; you attempt to excel yourself, press, and are lost.

(2) *Stamina*. It is no good hurdling ever so beautifully if you cannot stay the course in a race. There are of course many ways of getting strong and fit. Two of the best are exaggerated striding or knee-lifting (see p. 61) over 80 yards up to 220. Both of these exercises are hard work and should be done not more than twice a day at most.

(3) *Speed*. I said that it was not necessary to be able to run fast in order to hurdle well; but at the same time it is a good thing to develop what speed you have. The best way to do this is to run a 100 yards, starting quite slow and working up to an "all out" finish 30 yards, 35, 40, up to 50 yards, increasing the finish each day and never doing this more than twice an afternoon. In these "all out" efforts go only so fast that you can keep your arms and legs working together rhythmically and your balance well forward (see pp. 59–60).

A

A

B

B

HURDLING

The action of both arms and legs can be very clearly seen in 33-45. Notice how the body is kept perfectly straight ahead throughout the clearance. Many hurdlers twist from the hips towards the rear leg as it swings through, which shows that their rear hip is not flexible enough. Another common fault is that of dropping the knee of the rear leg immediately the foot has cleared the hurdle, instead of bringing it through for a full stride effort as in 41-44.

PLATE VII

In 46–60 the distance of the take-off is just 6 ft. from the hurdle and the landing just over 3 ft. These distances are about right. A take-off from further away would be liable to bring him down on top of the hurdle while a closer one would either make him hit the top of the hurdle with his leading leg, or avoid doing so by crooking it, or swinging it up sideways. Notice also the carriage of the body which is of the greatest importance. At the take-off it is dipped right forward till at one moment the chin almost touches the knee of the leading leg in 51. Thereafter it is gradually raised till the normal running angle is resumed in 59 and 60. Note the effective arm control in these two photos.

Hurdling technique. Technique may be acquired in two ways—in your bedroom and on the track. They are to my mind equally important, with slight odds on the former. As has been emphasized before, flexibility is an absolute necessity to the would-be hurdler, and the only way to become supple—or "subtle", as one boy would call it—is to do some of the following exercises *regularly* each night all the year round, if possible, or at least during the whole of each Sports term.

(1) Kick up hurdle-height straight to your front with the left leg and at the same time stretch vigorously forward and downwards with your right hand towards your left toe. Do this with either leg.

(2) Place your left heel on a table about hurdle-height and bend forward till you touch your knee with your chin, at the same time keeping your right leg straight (see Fig. 10, p. 39).

(3) Keeping your knees straight, bend down and touch your toes with your clenched fingers (see Figs. 6 and 7, p. 39). These three exercises will loosen your thigh muscles.

(4) Pick up your knee, as in Figs. 8 and 9, p. 39, swing it back six inches, and then bring it forward with a big knee-lift reaching out as far as you can to your front. This should be done religiously, as it is one of the best exercises for the hips, which have to be perfectly supple before you can hope to be a good hurdler (see also Fig. 39, p. 100 *infra*).

(5) Get into the position on the floor just as when you pass over the hurdle (as in Figs. 11 and 12, p. 39). The thighs should be at right-angles to each other and the body must be kept upright. First stretch forward with your right hand and touch the toes of your left foot (as in Fig. 13, p. 39); then with the right elbow try to draw a semicircle round the outside of your right knee (as in Fig. 14, p. 39). This also is a splendid exercise

for almost all the muscles which are most used in hurdling. At first the last movement will seem impossible, but it can be done with courage and perseverance.

(6) This is much the same as (4), except that the right knee is picked straight up to the front as high as possible towards the chin. Then, while you rise on the toe of the left leg, the right foot is shot out as far to the front as possible. This exercise gives poise and tends to lengthen the stride by strengthening the knee-lift muscles (see Fig. 18, p. 39).

(7) Lie on your back and raise your legs slowly up and down several times, keeping the knees straight and making a slight pause just off the ground without actually allowing them to rest (see Fig. 15, p. 39).

(8) Lie on your back, fold your arms, raise your body, and stretch forward till you can touch your knees with your chin (see Fig. 16, p. 39). The last two develop the stomach muscles, which are of great importance in keeping the body forward during the clearance of the hurdle.

(9) The knee-bend as in P.T., only keeping as far forward on the toes as possible. A good variation of this exercise is to do it on one leg at a time. This strengthens the toes and instep, which must be very powerful, as ideally you should go over a full flight of hurdles without once letting your heel come to the ground.

How to learn the action. Here I think it will be best to set down the various points in their order of importance from the beginner's point of view. The best preliminary exercise, both for the complete novice and also for the tried hurdler, at the beginning of each season consists in walking over a very low hurdle, exaggerating the action as much as possible. The first requirement is a hurdle with a knock-off top adjusted at least a foot lower than that over which the race will be run. Walk slowly up to the hurdle and swing the left (or leading) leg straight over it. Care should be taken to keep the knee unbent and not to get any sideway movement into the motion. The leg should resemble a pendulum, swinging cleanly from the hips at right-angles to the hurdle. As the left leg comes up, the right arm should reach forwards and downwards and an effort should be made to touch the toes of the left foot with the fingers of the right hand, while a sharp dip at the waist should bring the chin down to the left knee. As the foot of the left (or leading) leg comes to the ground on the further side of the hurdle, the weight should be transferred on to its toes and the rear (right) leg should be swung through sideways as high

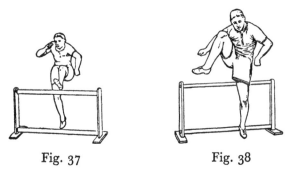

Fig. 37   Fig. 38

and "snappily" as possible. When the right knee has cleared the top of the hurdle, it should be forced upwards as far as it can go towards the chin, and the foot should be stretched ahead for as long a stride as possible. Care must be taken to keep the body well forward throughout the clearance.

This exercise is really splendid both for inculcating the main principles of style and also for more experienced performers who want a good stretch for their hurdling muscles at the beginning of the season. It has the effect of making the beginner, as it were, "slow motion" the clearance action, emphasizing and exaggerating all the points that matter most. The above exercise may be done with advantage as many as half a dozen times.

After this the hurdle may be taken at a slow run. Remember that you do not jump, but stride, over the hurdle. Try, then, not to spring at the take-off, or at least do not emphasize the bounding movement, otherwise you will most certainly "sail" rather than stride over the hurdle. Also you must be careful to trail your right or rear leg well behind you. It should not be swung through till the left (or leading) leg is over the hurdle and beginning to descend. One of the chief principles is that the legs should be kept as far apart as possible. Above all, they must not land together on the further side of the hurdle, for if they do the rhythm of the striding motion will be lost. The landing should be made on the toes and should in consequence be noiseless. You can often tell whether the hurdler has a good body-lean as he descends by the amount of noise he makes, for if he is on his toes he will almost certainly be well forward as well as being quiet.

Fig. 39

One of the most common failings among hurdlers, even in the first class, is a lack of flexibility in the hip of the take-off leg. The following is an exercise which is excellent for producing this. The hurdler walks up to the hurdle placing his leading leg just outside of it (see Fig. 39). Then he swings his take-off leg through just as he does in the actual hurdling clearance. He may at first assist this movement with his hand as in Fig. 39, but should try to do it without such an aid, as soon as he can. The chief thing to avoid is any sideway lean from the hips; the shoulders should be kept square to the front throughout. This exercise is useful both for training and also when "limbering up" before a race.

How much to do. It is a great mistake in training to run

over the full flight continually. The best plan is to start over one hurdle and perfect your style over one only; for if you can clear one really well, the rest will come fairly easily if you are fit. After you are happy over a single hurdle you can put up two or three, but not more. Once every other day run over five hurdles, or even the whole flight, in competition with someone a little faster than yourself. Whenever you go over hurdles, persuade a friend to watch for faults. Probably the best place to stand is some 30 yards to the side, as most of the faults can be detected from there. At the beginning of the season, when you are practising over a single hurdle, a committee of three or even four can watch the clearance with advantage, as it is extraordinarily hard to detect more than one fault at a time. No. 1 stands to the front, to see whether the leading leg comes up straight or not; No. 2 behind, to see whether the rear knee is swinging through high enough; No. 3 to the left side, to notice where the take-off and landing were made in relation to the positions of the paper; No. 4, who should have the most experience, stands on the right and notices the body-lean and the arm action.

The most useful "watcher" possible is a camera placed on a tripod on a level with the top of the hurdle. Action photographs are tremendously valuable in finding flaws in style, especially if they be compared with those in this book (see p. 143 in Appendix C).

General suggestions. Do not forget to practise the start and approach to the first hurdle till you can be certain of making a clean clearance. If you have great difficulty in doing the regulation "three strides" in between the hurdles, it will be best to do "fives", chopping your stride an inch or two if necessary. Never alternate with the take-off foot, which should always be the same. If a race is thrust upon you before you are really fit, but only if so, it will be well to get your confidence by going over the full flight once or twice a day in the week before, leaving, however, the last day for a rest. On the afternoon of a race always go through some loosening exercises and fly a few hurdles ten minutes or so beforehand. This will warm you up and ensure your getting into your stride at once.

In conclusion, remember that hurdling is an art, and he who would excel must take an artist's pride in attaining perfection without bothering too much about winning races; that will come later.

CHAPTER VIII

HIGH JUMPING

F EW athletic records strike the imagination with such force as the 6 ft. 8¼ in. set up by H. M. Osborne, the American Olympic champion, in 1924. If you watch the ordinary jumper at any school Sports, this record becomes yet more amazing. How can it be possible for any man jumping in this style, however full of spring, to clear upwards of 7 ft.? The answer of course is that he cannot. The old "scissors" style, in which the bar is cleared in a sitting position (see Pl. VIII, p. 104), has very rarely produced anything over 6 ft. and not often as high. Series C on Pl. X shows such a jumper failing at that height. Probably, had he learnt a more scientific method, he would have been capable of 6 ft. 4 in. or more.

What then is so wrong with the "scissors" method that it thus entails a loss of at least 4, if not 6, inches? In the first place, the jumper wastes a tremendous lot of energy by lifting his head and shoulders—the heaviest part of his anatomy—much higher than he need. In other words, there is no "lie-out". If you compare Series B and C on Pl. X this will at once be apparent. The scientific jumper manipulates his body in such a way that the loss of energy is cut down to a minimum, and any protruding portions dodge the cross-bar by a series of wriggles, kicks, and turns.

Secondly, the ordinary "scissors" jumper almost entirely fails to make use of leg-swing. In order to test the possibilities of this, catch hold of two ropes in a gymnasium, then kick as strongly as you can with both legs in quick succession. If you allow your body to go with the drive of your kicks, you will find that it is swung up into a horizontal position, though without any spring off either foot or pull up with the arms. Such is the power of leg-swing. The problem confronting the jumper is to combine swing simultaneously with spring. This is the basic principle of good high jumping and not at all easy to master.

At once the question arises whether high jumping can be learnt. The answer I believe to be emphatically "Yes!" Two examples will be sufficient to account for this optimism. H. M. Osborne, while at school, could do no better than 5 ft. 3 in. by the "scissors" method. He read an article on high jumping, changed his style, and promptly cleared 5 ft. 7¾ in. A few weeks later, with some coaching, he went up to 5 ft. 9¾ in., and early in the next season he was doing 6 ft. In my own experience I have had a boy of 15, who had done 4 ft. 6 in. jumping "scissors", clearing 5 ft. 1 in. after a month's coaching not more than twice—more often once—a week. Such instances could be multiplied.

In order to succeed it is almost essential—and certainly a hundred times more interesting—to understand what you are doing. Hence the excuse for a short treatise on the general principles of high jumping.

Unlike hurdling, where correct style is more or less cut and dried, there is a large number of styles in high jumping. Nevertheless, in order to withstand scientific criticism, they must obey certain principles, which I shall try to set forth below under their various headings.

THE APPROACH. The natural instinct is to increase the speed of the run as the heights become greater. It is true that a few have been successful with a fast approach. Generally speaking, however, this is a mistake, as the effort of converting the horizontal into a vertical impetus is so great that the leg-stamp at the take-off must be quite extraordinarily strong. Moreover, there is a considerable loss of energy when the jumper clears a distance of 14 or 15 ft. from take-off to landing.

Most of the greatest jumpers approach at a slow, springy trot, little, if at all, faster than a brisk walk and only quicken on the last two strides. Others actually walk up to the bar, and I believe that in training it is of the utmost importance to practise in this way. The speed and the length of the approach will depend on the physical attributes of the jumper, but I believe that *all* will benefit by a short, slow approach, at any rate in training—6 to 8 yards should be ample. Generally it is wise to measure your run-up carefully, so that it may become as mechanical as possible. The great thing is not to have to bother about it in competition; you can then concentrate entirely on the action of the jump.

THE TAKE-OFF. Ideally the jumper should take off as close to the bar as possible. This distance may be best found by standing and kicking up with your leading leg so that you just miss the bar with it; your take-off should then be a few inches back. In training put down a bit of white cardboard and aim to hit it with your spikes as you take off. Most will find that they take off much too far away. The faster the approach, the stronger will this tendency be. On Plate IX notice No. 27 of Simmons and contrast it with X, A 1 of Van Geyzel. Probably the latter's chief fault is an over-quick approach; hence he takes off over 4 ft. away from the bar. Simmons, in No. 14, is only 3 ft. from the bar. His jump is therefore much more of a spring straight up into the air, whereas Van Geyzel combines a miniature long jump with his height clearance and thus wastes energy.

The actual spring from the take-off leg consists of a tremendous stamp, in the course of which the foot is absolutely flat for a fraction of a second (see Pls. VIII, 7 and IX, 33); many coaches, in fact, advise putting the heel down *first*. In order to get full benefit from the drive, the body should be as far forward as the action of the leading leg will allow (see below, p. 113). Some jumpers believe in clipping the last two strides short, so as to insure getting the body forward (see Chapter IV on "Running", p. 50).

THE CLEARANCE. (a) *Leading leg action.* I do not at the moment intend to discuss any special style of jump; my concern here is with principles. It has been pointed out above that height should be gained by a combination of swing and spring. Some jumpers will emphasize one, some the other; this will depend on their physique. The more natural spring a man has, the more will he tend to neglect the swing. On the other hand, the heavier a jumper is, the more will he profit from the pendulum-like action of the legs, which are themselves by no means light. Howard Baker, holder of the English record at 6 ft. 5 in., weighed about 14 stone, and Landon, the Olympic winner in 1920, always said that if he had weighed a stone more he could have added several inches to his jump. Both of these jumped in the "turn-in-the-air" style, where the full benefit of the leg-swing can be used to best advantage. The heavy-weights *must* swing to be successful; their lighter, smaller *confrères* may rely more on spring. A man like Lewden, who stands 5 ft. 8 in. and has cleared 6 ft. 5⅞ in., must have made use of both to their fullest degree in order to put up such an astounding performance.

Whether the swing of a leg is powerful or not may be judged by its angle. If the effort has been really vigorous, it is bound to be straight. If you compare Pls. VIII, 1 and IX, 37 (over bar), the contrast is obvious.

In all forms of high jumping a straight powerful swing-up with the leading leg is a fundamental. It should come from the hip, just as in kicking a football, and the knee should be perfectly stiff and unflexed from the moment after it has cleared the ground and passed the take-off leg. Nos. 27–29 and 33–35 on Pl. IX illustrate this well; but it will be noticed that the other jumpers illustrated lack the power which Simmons puts into his leg-swing. Probably it is very largely owing to this that he has cleared 6 ft. 2 in. at the age of 17.

The function of the rear leg will be dealt with later on in the chapter, when the various forms of jumping are analysed.

(b) *The lie-out.* Obviously the position in Pl. VIII, 1 is highly unsatisfactory, and the gain from a lie-out, as in Pl. VIII, 6 and 11 or Pl. IX, 26 and 37, is equally apparent. There are many types of lie-out. Jumpers go over the bar on their backs, sides, or fronts; some lean forward, some flick their body out straight; everything depends on the style of the particular individual. The one position which *no* jumper who has any pretence to a scientific form will adopt is the sitting one, as on Pl. X and Pl. VIII, 1.

The type of lie-out must be governed by the following rule, which the jumper is advised to read carefully and so order his action that the judges may not have the least excuse for disqualifying him. "Neither diving nor somersaulting over the bar shall be permitted. A fair jump is one where the head of the contestant does not go over the bar before the feet, and is not below the buttocks in clearing the bar."

(c) *The landing* (see p. 20 on the necessity for good, big pits with plenty of sand in them). The unskilled performer who achieves a lie-out may find it a painful business, as, unless he can manage some kind of a twist or turn after or during his clearance, he will descend on his back with a bump. The polished jumper will always manage to land on his feet or on his hands and feet, often most gracefully (see Pl. X, A, 10–12).

THE THREE MAIN STYLES OF HIGH JUMPING

Having dealt with the principles of all successful jumping, I will proceed to analyse, more or less in detail, the three styles of which all others are really modified forms. These are (1) the "scissors", (2) the "Western Roll", and (3) the "turn-in-the-air" styles. I have set them down in what I believe to be their order of difficulty.

(1) *The "scissors"*. It is true that I have riddled this style with criticism, but in doing so I had in mind the type of hopelessness shown on Pl. VIII, 1. I did not mean to imply that a modified form of "scissors" cannot be quite effective. The angle of approach should be about 45°. The jumper should concentrate on the following points: (i) a slow run-up; (ii) a take-off as close to the bar as possible; (iii) a combination of spring and swing to get height; (iv) a lie-out either on his back or side.

Larsen, the American, used the "scissors" style with a lie-out. He went over the bar almost flat on his back, and at the moment of clearance, having taken off from the left foot, he whipped his right arm downwards, causing his body to roll over towards the landing pit, into which he descended on his hands and feet. If you can imagine the jumper on Pl. VIII, 1 lying flat on his back over the bar with his legs straight out in front of him, you will see the effect of Larsen's arm action in bringing about a comfortable landing. Larsen, it is true, is one of the very few men who have been successful with a fast approach, but I believe that his type of lie-out and partial turn might be used just as well with a slower run-up. Certainly it would be easier to time, owing to the slower movement of the action. This type of jump might be useful for those who do not care to embark on either of the other two forms, which need some time to learn.

(2) *The "Western Roll"*. Put in a nutshell, this form

depends on an approach from the side, a take-off from the foot nearest the bar, and a tremendous swing-up with the outside foot. Thereafter there are two types of action used by great jumpers. The simplest, though not the most scientific, is that of King, winner of the Olympic event in 1928, illustrated on Pl. VIII, 2–6. In this type of jump there is a continuous curl in the air, which is caused by the action of the outside leading leg. The jumper goes over sideways in a curled-up position. There is no arm or leg action in mid-air, and the danger-point is the hip, as no provision is made for drawing it away from the bar, as in other more scientific forms.

Its merit lies in its simplicity. When once the take-off with the "wrong foot" is mastered, it is fairly plain sailing. Care should be taken to keep the body forward during the ascent, for if it be allowed to draw backwards there will be a serious loss of balance. Look at Pl. VIII, 2–4; notice how the body is kept forward, as also in 7, 8, and 10. Beginners will probably find difficulty with the action of the take-off leg; this should be delayed till the leading foot has reached the level of the bar. Compare Nos. 3 (b) and 9 with 18 and 19. In the latter pair there is a tendency to hurry the swing-up with the take-off leg, whose function is to carry on the lifting process when the leading leg has expended its force.

The other modification of the "Western Roll" is a much more economical style, though more difficult to perfect. Instead of clearing the cross-bar in a hunched-up position, the body and legs are flicked out into a straight line, so that the jumper is lying sideways over the bar, as in Pl. VIII, 11. The danger of this jump is that if the body is not straightened out, *i.e.* if there is any lean forward from the waist, the chance of disqualification will be considerable. If you examine No. 11 you will see that the rule is not contravened, for the feet are crossing the bar before the head, and the buttocks are lower than it. In No. 12, however, it is quite a different matter. This was taken a fraction of a second later, showing the arm action and its result. Just as the body is centred over the bar, the left hand is swung sharply downwards and backwards. The roll-over action, begun by the leading leg, is thus accelerated and the left hip drawn away from the bar. This action may also be noticed in No. 17, though in both cases the timing is a fraction late. Incidentally it may be seen how this movement tended to hold the bar against the uprights, though originally that was not its aim. In consequence of the unfair advantage gained by jumpers in this style the International Olympic Committee decided that the cross-bar should rest on a square bracket on the inside of the uprights. Compare No. 14 with 16, and the difference between the new and old supports will be plain. Nevertheless, despite this change, the "Western Roll", especially the second type, has a great deal to commend it, and it has been used successfully under the new conditions.

(3) *The "turn-in-the-air"*. Personally I am inclined to favour the "turn-in-the-air" as being the most polished type of jump when perfection of style is attained; but really there is very little in it, and the choice will be mainly a matter of physical qualifications.

The "turn-in-the-air" style—in America it is called the "Eastern form"—demands great flexibility and perfect muscular condition. Especially must the jumper be able to kick his own height with either leg. H. A. Simmons is perhaps extraordinary in his suppleness. He can kick 6 ft. 7 in., though only 5 ft. 10 in. in height (see No. 20), and his general flexibility will be in little doubt after an examination of No. 19.

The approach for this type of jump is straight from the front. The take-off foot should be put down absolutely square, *i.e.* at 90° to the bar. The kick-up with the leading leg should be as strong as possible, with a stiff knee, as in Nos. 14–16 and 22–24. A bent leg means a lack of vigour in the kick (see Nos. 1 and 2). The ankle and toes of the leading foot should be twisted inwards in the direction in which the turn will be made; this will be to the left if the take-off is from the left foot, and *vice versa*.

The kick-up with the leading leg is a fundamental of this jump and is the first thing to be mastered, for without it no great heights will ever be attained. It can best be tackled by jumping with an approach of one or two strides only. The most difficult thing for beginners to learn is the combination of springing from the take-off foot and simultaneously swinging up with the other.

The arm action also is of importance in aiding the upward impulse. Simmons is peculiar in this respect, as he flings up both hands at the take-off. A study of action photographs of many jumpers reveals the fact that they all manipulate their arms differently at this moment. Any generalization on the point is therefore unwise, though probably the arm on the opposite side to the leading leg drives up with it, while the other arm flies up in sympathy with the power of the movement in order to maintain the balance of the body.

The swing of the take-off leg is, as in the other styles, a delayed action and should only begin when the foot of the leading leg is on a level with the cross-bar (see Pl. IX, 24–26 and 35–37). When it does begin it should come straight from the hips, with, if possible, a straight leg and every ounce of power available. The direction of the kick will have to be a trifle sideways; otherwise the bar will be knocked off (see Fig. 40).

As regards the lie-out, the twist of the leading foot will impart a slight turn to the body as it rises to the bar. Notice that the lie-out does not occur until the swing of the take-off leg reaches its maximum height (see Pl. IX, 22–26, 27–31 and Pl. X, A). At this moment the jumper should be lying sideways over the bar, as in Pl. IX, 30 or 37. The hips have not yet crossed, and the problem is how to draw them away from the bar. If this can be done in such a way that the stomach is next to the bar instead of the protruding hip-bone, there will be a clear gain of several inches.

In order to do this, the body must be turned, and there are several ways of achieving this. The head may be twisted round to the left, and likewise the hips from the waist. The left arm may be swung back. Lastly and most effective, especially if in co-operation with some or all of the others, the left leg may be kicked backwards and

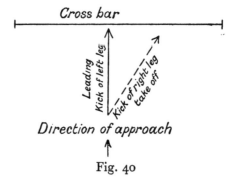

Fig. 40

downwards. The result of this will be to turn the hips away from the bar, substituting the presumably flat surface of the stomach, and to drop the legs and raise the body in such a way that a landing is made on the feet facing the bar and quite close to it.

Timing this turn correctly is the most difficult thing about the jump, and very few have managed it. Especially if the run-up is a fast one, the task of bringing off the turn at the right fraction of a second becomes well-nigh impossible. In Series A on Pl. X this is the main fault. The turn should have been completed during 6 and 7 in order to draw the hips away from the bar. Actually the only benefit gained from the turn was a safe and graceful landing.

26	25	24
32	31	30
38	37	36

THE TURN-IN-THE-AIR STYLE

R. Hodges (2nd, Olympic Games, 6 ft. 3¼ in.) 21–26, jumps in the turn-in-the-air style. Note position of the leading leg at the take-off and compare it with 28 and 34. The left arm is driving upwards; the right is maintaining the balance of the body. (2) Examine the delayed action of the take-off leg in 21–25, when it is just beginning to swing up. (3) The timing of the lie out is also very clearly shown in 22, 24, 25 and 26.

H. A. Simmons, 27–38, who is the first English schoolboy to clear over 6 ft. His extreme suppleness (see Exercises 32 and 38) make him ideally suited to the turn-in-the-air style. So steeply can he swing up with his leading leg that he can take-off very close to the bar (see 27, 28, 33 and 34). His leg action in rising to the bar is excellent: note the straightness of his leading leg (27–29, 34–36) and also the height reached with his take-off leg in 30

PLATE IX

and 36 where he is jumping 6 ft. Whether he can yet time that elusive turn I do not know. 31 is no indication, as he was jumping at a low height under bad conditions and there is a consequent lack of power noticeable in the leg action. 30 and 37 show that critical stage when the thigh is centred over the bar and the left foot must be cut downwards and backwards in order to draw the left hip away from the bar. This brings the body into an upright position away from the bar but makes for a landing close to it. Simmons' lie out differs from that of Hodges in that he leans forward from the waist whereas Hodges leans back. This is mainly a matter of physical differences. The lean forward requires considerably more flexibility but would seem to give better body balance and more control for any mid-air action.

Now in order to bring off this down-and-backwards-kick, the body must be raised a trifle above the bar. Pl. IX, 26, 30, 37 show the maximum lie-out possible for this type of jump. Experts lay down the angle as 30°. In other words, the jumper cannot get the maximum lie-out which the "Western Roll" form allows. On the other hand, the jumper, if he is skilful, does get the benefit of a full swing-up effort with *both* legs, whereas the "Western Roller" can only use maximum power with his leading leg. If he were to kick equally strongly with the second, the roll-over motion would be checked and the point of the action lost. There is one other disadvantage of this jump. In order to get the swing up to the bar with the leading leg, the jumper is inclined to assume a slightly backward position at the moment of taking off (see Pl. IX, 33), whereas the "Western Roller", leading with his outside foot, is further away from the bar with it and is thus able to get right over his take-off foot at the moment of impact (see Pl. VIII, 7).

HINTS ON TRAINING. So much, then, for the various types of action. The question is how to learn to improve your own performance in the rather limited time at your disposal. Probably, of all the events, high jumping, scientifically carried out, requires the most perfect muscular condition. It follows, then, that a great deal can be done by means of indoor exercise. High kicking is of course essential. Do not overdo this at first, and always start your work gently; otherwise you run the risk of a torn muscle. There are two modifications of the ordinary high-kicking exercise, both of which are most valuable. The first consists in kicking up with the leading leg as high as possible and at the same time springing off the take-off leg. It is not an easy thing to do and care must be taken not to land on the back of your head. At the same time it is infinitely worth while mastering, as it develops the power of combining swing with spring, which is the greatest asset a high jumper can have. The interest will be increased if some mark is put up to hit with your leading leg; this should be a few inches higher than you can kick without the spring. In this way you will be able to measure your progress.

The second exercise aims at giving the knack of the double kick used in the "scissors" and "turn-in-the air" styles. Kick up with your leading leg and follow it up immediately with a kick with your take-off leg, but without any spring off it. Here again the greatest care must be taken not to topple over backwards, unless something soft is there to receive you. The value of the exercise lies in the fact that it teaches you to keep your body forward as you kick and so will help to overcome the beginner's tendency to a premature lie-out.

Hopping exercises are useful for developing the foot-stamp of the take-off leg. Here again it may be emphasized that the spring can never produce its full power unless the heel comes to the ground; therefore in doing the hopping exercises exaggerate this point.

Other exercises which are of use to the high jumper will be found on pages 38–41; they are Nos. 1–3, 5, 7–11, 13.

PRACTISING THE JUMP. The details of jumping styles given above sound highly alarming, if not impossible, to the ordinary being. And so they would be if anyone attempted to deal with the whole action straight away. Very few boys, for instance, could tackle the "turn-in-the-air" action in all its details while at school—they have not the time. Fortunately it is possible to start with fundamentals and graft on the refinements of mid-air arm and leg action later. I have analysed it briefly here to show what it is, so that if any enthusiasts start out to learn it they may know what their goal is.

Here, then, I will try to set out the fundamentals in the order in which they should be tackled.

(1) Take two steps only and practise swinging up to

the bar with your leading leg. Go right through with your swing and do not bother very much about the spring or swing-up of your take-off leg—if it knocks the bar off, what matter so long as the leading leg has soared triumphantly above it? Do this three or four times only, with the bar at a height that you can normally clear comfortably.

(2) Try to combine the swing of your leading leg with a spring from your take-off; but do not bother about swinging up with the take-off foot.

(3) The next step is to add the swing-up with your take-off leg. Remember that this should be a delayed action, though at low heights, of necessity, the pause cannot be long. You should aim at a full swing-up, so that the foot will reach a level higher than the leading leg (see Pl. IX, 30, 37, and X, B 7). Keep in mind that the test of power is an unflexed knee; the leg should swing up pendulum-wise from the hip.

(4) Finally comes the turn. Do not forget, however, that the turn is a refinement and not an essential of the style. It will in fact do three things for you. You will land on your feet facing the bar; you will gain several inches in height if your timing is correct; and last, but by no means least owing to the vanity in human nature, the appearance of your jump will be improved tremendously.

Most novices beginning this jump think that the turn is the one essential. When they try to do it they get the motive power by putting down the take-off foot sideways. Bear in mind that the turn does *not* come from the take-off foot at all. It is begun by the inward twist of the leading foot and completed by the kick of the take-off foot, on which the landing is made (see Series A, Pl. X). It cannot be too strongly urged that the steps detailed above should be taken one by one. No useful purpose will be served by trying to do the turn until the follow-up kick with the take-off leg has been tackled.

Do not do a lot of "all out" jumping in practice, though one or two (not more) attempts at height may be made at the end of each practice. Generally the bar should be put just as high as you can comfortably clear. It is moreover extremely unwise to overdo things. Make a hard and fast rule that you will limit yourself to a definite number of jumps, which should certainly not exceed a dozen; if competition is anywhere near, half that number will be ample.

One of the greatest difficulties in learning this jump is that in order to get a lie-out and do the turn in the air, the clearance must be over a considerable height. This, however, does not alter the fact that for training purposes the bar should be comparatively low, as continual jumping over maximum heights will very soon take all the spring out of the muscles. The solution of the difficulty seems to lie in a mastery of the first three steps, by which time the comfortable clearance height will be sufficient to permit getting in both lie-out and turn; but until the full swing-up with the take-off leg can be done successfully it is a great mistake to try to turn, as it is almost bound to weaken the action of that leg in attempting to kick under before the top of its swing has been reached.

So far I have been mainly concerned with the "scissors" and "turn-in-the-air" forms; the same principles largely apply to both. In the "Western Roll" form the first problem is the take-off, which is made from the foot nearest the bar. This will best be learnt by putting the bar at a low height and practising jumping off the inside foot, emphasizing at the same time the swing-up of the outside leg and the inside arm (see Pl. VIII, 3 a, 8, 14). As in the other forms, the full swing-up of the leading leg is of the greatest importance; it should aim at a point beyond the bar. Care should be taken to see that the body does not lie back. It should be well over the take-off foot at the moment of impact, and the lie-out should not begin until the take-off leg is half way up to the bar (see Pl. VIII, 3 a–6). Whether the jumper adopts the continuous curling jump (1–6) or straightens out his body over the bar (7–12) will depend on himself; the merits of each are discussed above and the details of the action are given there.

Much the same methods may be applied to this style as those given above, though in this case the first two steps may with advantage be combined into one—the spring and swing can be learnt together. Next, attention should be concentrated on the *delayed* action of the take-off leg, as there is a strong tendency to hurry it; Pl. VIII, 17, 18 and 19 show this to a certain extent.

SUMMARY. It is possible for a jumper to teach himself, but if a friend will watch for faults, the work will be infinitely easier and the progress much more rapid. He should stand about 30 yards away, and I give here briefly the points to look out for.

From the side: (1) the distance of (*a*) the take-off, and (*b*) the landing from the bar; (2) the straightness of the leading leg as it comes up to the bar; (3) the same for the take-off leg, and also whether the action is sufficiently delayed; (4) the body-angle at the moment of take-off; (5) the timing of the lie-out; (6) the timing of the turn.

From behind: (1) Whether the heel is coming to the ground as it should at the foot-stamp of the take-off; (2) the action of the take-off leg in its following-up swing.

From the front: (1) That the take-off foot is square to the front; (2) that the swing of the leading leg is straight; (3) the timing of the lie-out.

These are most of the things which need attention in the "turn-in-the-air" style, but be it noted that only one can be watched at once. If you want the ideal critic, call in the camera (see "Photography in Athletics" in Appendix C).

COMPETITIVE HINTS.

(1) A complete rest of two or three days from all jumping should be taken before competition.

(2) Keep your legs as warm as possible in between the jumps; cold, stiff muscles will take inches off your jump.

(3) See that your shoes fit really tightly; sloppily fitting shoes are one of the worst enemies of good jumping.

(4) Before you begin jumping always run through some stretching exercises, do some high kicking, and jog a short distance round the track to get your muscles loosened and warmed up.

(5) Do not necessarily start jumping at the low heights if you are certain you can clear them. It is a waste of energy and you may want it all at the bigger heights (see rule (f), p. 149 in Appendix D).

(6) Success in high jumping is very much a matter of determination and confidence; therefore cultivate these mental qualities (see Appendix B, p. 140).

(7) Some jumpers put a handkerchief upon the bar, but it is much better to be able to do without such aids. If for any reason you cannot hang your handkerchief, you will be handicapped should you have been used to it in practice.

(8) Get in the way of asking yourself, when you have failed, why you did so. Those who do great things in this event are they who can best analyse their own form.

CHAPTER IX

LONG JUMPING

Dᴜʀɪɴɢ the past few years there has been a great advance in long jumping. Before the War 23 ft. was considered a wonderful performance, but of late 25 ft. has been surpassed quite a number of times in America. It is true that negroes have done much of the big jumping, and it is possible that their feet may be better suited for this event; but so considerable has been the increase in standard that one is driven to the conclusion that an improvement in skill must have played a considerable part therein.

In order to see how this may be so, I will try to split up the technique of long jumping into its component parts. These are (1) the run-up, (2) the take-off, (3) the flight, (4) the landing.

The run-up. The first essential of successful long jumping is speed in the approach. It has been said that anyone capable of running a hundred yards in under 11 seconds should be capable of clearing 20 ft., *if he can get his run-up right.* This brings me to the most crucial point. A long jumper must be capable of hitting the board, which may have a maximum width of 8 inches (see rule (*a*), p. 150 in Appendix D), travelling his fastest at the end of a run-up which may vary from 25 to 40 yards. Moreover he should not only hit the board but be as near as possible to the far, *i.e.* the pit, edge of it.

Obviously if he is going to do this, he has got to be striding extremely evenly. Now when anyone begins training, his running is almost always lacking in regularity (see Fig. 34). It is urged therefore that he who wishes to take up long jumping should do plenty of running first and especially concentrate on the sprint action (see pp. 54–61); otherwise he will waste a lot of time in finding a run-up which will only prove quite wrong the next time that he turns out.

What the length of the approach should be will depend on the physique of the jumper. The big, strong sprinter will benefit from a long run-up, *i.e.* 40 yards, but those with less stamina will only tire themselves before they arrive at the take-off board if they use the long run-up.

It should not be assumed from the above generalization that the run-up is an "all out" effort from start to take-off. The idea is to choose such a length of approach as will allow acceleration to full speed at the moment of hitting the board. When once the approximate length is

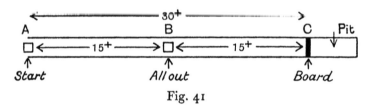

Fig. 41

decided on, the following method will be found excellent for determining the exact distance.

Suppose that you decide on 30 yards as your approximate distance. Stride this out from the take-off board and put down a piece of white cardboard at that point on the track (*A* in Fig. 41). Then pace out 15 yards towards the take-off and put down another piece of cardboard at that point (*B* in diagram). In order to find your correct distance you will have to get two friends to watch where your feet strike at *B* and *C* in the diagram. From *A* to *B* you will increase your speed, aiming to hit *B* with your take-off foot. At the moment of passing *B* you break into an "all out" sprint action. Now comes the important thing to remember. When you are trying to get your run-up, you must take no notice of the board whatever. Run straight over it *and* the pit without

THE LONG JUMP

These series show the walk-in-the-air jump in which the jumper continues his running for three strides and at the completion of the third shoots out both legs for a landing. Honner, himself, stresses the importance of the knee lift in each of these (see 3, 10, 15). The jump, made without a proper take-off board, is not a good specimen of Honner's jumping, but it does show very clearly how strong the stomach muscles need to be. Contrast positions 13 and 22 to see how the body is drawn from a backward into a forward angle by their unaided agency in mid-air.

Here is the take-off and first two of the strides. Notice the foot "roll" at the take-off when the foot is flat for an instant (28–29) till it leaves the ground with a strong toe and ankle flick which lends speed to the upward impetus. When Honner is in his best form the knee lift of the leading leg (left) and the accompanying upward drive of the right arm are

PLATE XI

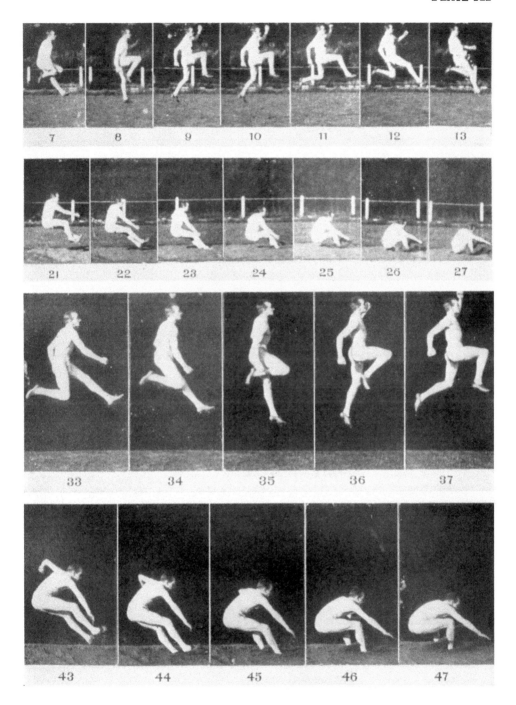

more vigorous than those shown here. This is a point upon which every jumper should concentrate in practice—at first with a slow run up. The action of the take-off leg, whether in this or the ordinary "sail" flight, should be a trifle delayed.

A perfect landing demands that both arms should be behind the body at the moment the feet strike the pit. When this is achieved, the jumper can afford a more backward body angle at the moment of landing, as he has the pendulum forward swing of the arms to help bring his body forward so that he falls forward and not back. This is also done by allowing the knees to flex (see 43–47) so that the forward momentum of the body is not thrown backwards by the shock of landing. The jumper should thus tumble straight forward on to his hands and knees.

attempting to jump or in any way checking the rhythm of your running.

You then find out from your friends where your feet hit at B and C. Suppose you were 1 foot over the board with your take-off foot, but hit B with it, all you have to do is to move B and A 12 inches back and try again.

To take another example, if you hit B with your wrong foot and were 3 ft. short of the board, you might experiment by putting A back a yard and B forward the same distance.

This method is not difficult to work, but two points need emphasizing. You should get your friends, watching B and C, to stand well back, say 10 or 15 yards, so that they may have a chance of getting a clear sight of your leg action; if they are too close they cannot. Tell them also to mark the position of your foot immediately you have passed.

When you have definitely fixed the positions of A and B, measure them with a tape, so that you may be certain of finding them in the future. Do not, however, think that all your troubles are at an end in so far as the run-up is concerned. Wind, weather, and personal conditions are always altering, so that you will have to learn by experience what allowance to make. A wind against or a very slow track may demand that A and B both be moved forward 12 inches or so, while a following wind will have an opposite effect.

As has been said above, the sprint action should be used, and it is of the utmost importance, first, to get a really good forward lean of the body, and, secondly, to exaggerate the knee-lift. Especially at the last two or three strides before reaching the board is it essential that the balance should be perfect and the weight of the body well over the foot as it lands. Pl. XI, A 1 and B 28 both show a fault in this respect. If great difficulty be found in getting the necessary forward body-angle at this point, it may be advisable to clip these strides a few inches; but if so there will probably be difficulty about hitting the board, and the normal sprinting stride, which already should be slightly shortened, ought to be kept, if possible. Should the run-up be inaccurate, there will be a loss of at least a foot, for if the jumper has to stretch out to the board, he cannot get any power into his take-off with a backward body-angle, and if he has to shorten his stride he will lose momentum as well as making a poor take-off through lack of balance (see Pl. XV, A).

The take-off. This, as in high jumping, consists of a powerful foot-stamp, in which the heel hits the ground with considerable force. In order to get the maximum effect from the spring, the body must be poised and well forward. Just as in high jumping, if a slightly crouching position be adopted during the last few strides, as well as at the moment of taking off, more power will be imparted to the foot-stamp.

The best way to develop the foot-stamp in practice is to take a short run of ten yards, concentrating entirely on form at the take-off. Emphasis should be laid on the downward pull of the opposite arm, which governs the leg drive—see Pl. XI, A 2 and XI, B 29, in which the right leg is taking off and the left hand pulled downwards and backwards. Simultaneously the other leg is forced forwards and upwards with every available ounce of energy and as big a knee-lift as possible. This action of the leading leg is of the greatest importance, whatever type of flight be adopted. It should be practised assiduously with the short run-up, and every effort should be made to put as much drive as possible in both this and the stamp of the take-off leg. Notice on Pl. XI, A, 3 and 4, B, 30 and 31 that the opposite arm, punched upwards, is helping this knee-lift. These two movements decide both the height to which the jumper will rise and thus ultimately the distance of his clearance.

The flight. There are two types of flight. In one the jumper draws his feet up under him with his knees tucked up towards his chin. In the other he carries on his running action in mid-air, as shown in Pl. XI, 1–27. What the respective merits of these styles are I find it very hard to say. The majority of the best modern jumpers use the second or some modification of it. I asked the opinion of E. B. Ham, who himself uses it and won the Olympic event at Amsterdam in 1928 with a jump of 25 ft. 4¼ in. He said he reckoned it gave him an extra 8 inches, because it got him into a better position for landing. D. H. Hubbard, another American, who holds the World's Record of 25 ft. 10⅞ in., reckons that it is worth more than this to him.

Obviously it is unwise to be dogmatic. If anyone wishes to tackle it, the best way to go about it is to practise with the short run-up. The action as carried out by Dr Honner, who is shown in Pl. XI, consists in carrying on the running action in mid-air. Three steps are taken, and at each there is a vigorous knee-lift (see 2, 9, and 15), till finally the legs are shot out for the landing.

The other style consists in following up the swing of the leading with that of the take-off leg, drawing the knees well into the chest, which should be pressed down towards them so that the body has a forward lean. The arms will fly upwards during the first half of the flight, but just before landing should be drawn forwards and downwards, thereby helping the body to keep its forward poise. The legs should be together and the whole position balanced, so that the landing may be made to the best advantage. The follow-up action of the take-off leg should not be hurried. Just as in the high jump, it is delayed until the drive of the leading leg has expended most of its power.

The landing. This is where the expert gains over the

novice. There is perhaps as much as 2 ft. difference between a scientific landing and a haphazard one. It is recommended that the following type of landing be practised with the slow, short run-up.

Just as the legs are descending into the pit they should be shot out ahead of the body as in Pl. XI, A, 22, 43. The body will be thrown into a more or less upright position by this manœuvre, and as the feet strike the sand the arms should swing behind the body. In order to prevent falling backwards the knees should flex, as in Pl. XI, B, 45–47, only more so, and at the same moment both arms are swung forward unflexed, bringing the body with them. The jumper then falls straight forward on to his hands and knees. In making his landing the jumper should relax his leg muscles, so that the break-at-the-knee movement may be possible and also in order that the jar of landing may be lessened.

THE ESSENTIALS OF TRAINING. Just as in high jumping, it is entirely fatal to overdo the jumping in practice. It is such a temptation, if you are jumping well, to say to yourself, "One more, and I shall beat my own record!" or, if you have been unsuccessful, to go on in hopes that you may do better "later on". The only sound plan is to be methodical and strong-minded. Allow yourself, say, half a dozen jumps with the short run and three "all out" efforts with the full run. Make up your mind to practise some definite part of the action. You might concentrate on the take-off for the first three jumps and on the landing for the second three. Then in your "all out" jumps try to combine them. Three or four half-hours a week is plenty of time to spend on your jumping. Moreover, if you seem to lack spring, do not be afraid to rest; it is the only way to get it back. You should do no jumping at all for two, or better three, days before competition—that is essential.

Try to get a friend to train with you. It adds to the

fun and also you can watch each other for faults of form. Do not, however, think too much about making much distance in training. If you concentrate on doing things correctly, the length will come automatically when you come to jump in competition.

Muscular condition of course plays a great part in this event, and exercises should be done in order to improve this. The following of the exercises on pp. 38–41 are recommended: (*a*) to develop knee-lift and balance, Nos. 2, 10, 11; (*b*) as a leg strengthener, No. 9, especially the more advanced variation; (*c*) for the stomach, Nos. 7 and 8, both very important for the long jumper.

CHAPTER X

PUTTING THE WEIGHT

THE idea is very widely spread in England that this event is a slow, dull business, relegated to the heavy-weights who cannot achieve success in any other sphere of athletics. Certainly it cannot be denied that most of the successful weight-putters have been big men. Ralph Rose, for example, stood nearly 6 ft. 6 in. and weighed upwards of 20 stone. With this enormous size and strength he combined extremely fine style; hence his World's Record of 51 ft. made in 1909 has only lately been beaten in America.

The fact that style counts more than strength may be seen at any sports meeting where this event is held. In many ways it resembles boxing, where it is not always the biggest man who has the strongest punch. Jimmy Wilde, though weighing very little over 7 stone, is said to have had the punch of a 10-stone man. Knox, the famous Canadian all-round athlete, though weighing only 11 stone, put the weight 46 ft. How is it that these two men in their different ways could produce such wonderful power? The answer is two-fold. They combined speed with the knack of getting all their limited weight behind the drive of their arm.

Now it is in the achievement of these two things that success in shot-putting depends, and this is the purpose of each detail of the action which has been, and is still being, evolved by experts. The co-ordination of the various parts of the "put" requires a great deal of practice, and the enthusiasm necessary to cut out gradually from methods whatever tends to a loss of these two essentials, speed and power. That weight-putting is far from dull is proved for me by the fact that when I was

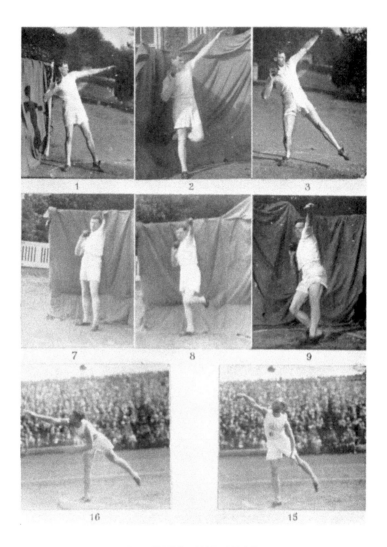

PUTTING THE SHOT

These composite photos 1–12 are an attempt on the part of the author to pose the style, which incorporates the latest evolution of form amongst the Scandinavian and American putters. Note: (1) elbow away from side in an under-behind the shot position; (2) the landing in 3 on the right leg followed almost simultaneously by a crouch on that leg and a bend back from the waist which should be more exaggerated in 4. In 5 the right arm and leg make a straight line as they should in a well co-ordinated put. The reverse of feet has been effected in 6 and the body is leaning after the shot.

Taken from the right front. Notice that the shot and right arm are just in sight the whole way across the ring in 9 and 10, but that the shot is kept snugly

PLATE XII

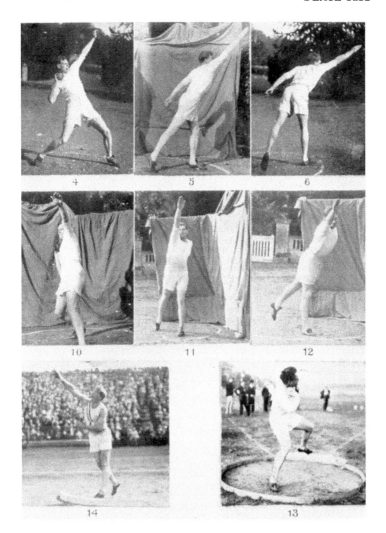

into the neck till the moment between 10 and 11, when it is driven upwards in a continuation of the line of arm and leg in 5. In 11 the eyes are following the shot in its upward flight.

In 13, R. L. Howland (Cambridge University and Achilles Club) has been caught in the middle of his spring across the ring. Note: (a) the closeness of the right foot to the ground and (b) the position of the right hand containing the shot. In 14, H. Brix (U.S.A., 2nd, 1928 Olympic Games, 51 ft. 8¼ in.) has just delivered the shot and has begun the reverse. He is following the shot with his eyes and there is every indication of a powerful finger flick. 15 shows R. S. Woods a fraction of a second later on in the reverse: here also it is evident that both fingers and wrist have played their part. In 16 Brix is finishing his reverse, leaning well after the shot and is in a finely poised position.

up at Cambridge the keenest section of the athletes was undoubtedly composed of those who were tackling this event.

THE ACTION ANALYSED. The action may be split up into (1) the preliminary stance; (2) the spring across the ring; (3) the put; (4) the reverse and follow-through.

(1) *The Preliminary Stance.* The putter stands sideways-on to the direction in which he will travel across the ring. The feet are about 18 inches apart, with the weight slightly more on the right than the left. The shot should rest in the lower joints of the fingers of the right hand; this will enable the fingers to impart a final flick to the shot as it leaves the hand. Some, however, may not be strong enough in the fingers to hold the shot in this way, and for them it will be best to let it drop down an inch into the palm of the hand.

The hand containing the shot is then tucked into the angle made between the neck and the collar-bone. Some putters keep the elbow pressed into the side. Practically all the best performers, however, hold the elbow away from the body (see Pl. XII, 1, 3, 4), as this gives the best drive effect when the arm comes into action with its weight right behind the shot. Notice, however, that this does not occur till the spring across the ring has been completed; for until that moment (see (4)) the putting arm remains quiescent in the position described.

The left arm should be used as a balancer to offset the weight of the shot and also to aid in the initial movement across the ring. It should be held about shoulder-high, as in 1.

The chief thing to remember about this preliminary position is that it should be relaxed and perfectly balanced. There should *not* be any crouch, *i.e.* a throwing upwards of the left arm with a bent right leg, as this position causes tension and detracts from speed of the movement across the ring.

(2) *The Spring across the Ring.* Some begin this movement by kicking upwards with a stiff left leg. R. S. Woods does it to perfection; but this pendulum swing is thought to be unwieldy, causing a lack of balance, and, unless the man be extraordinarily well poised naturally, this probably is so. The majority rely on a method which is less artistic, but generates speed without upsetting the balance.

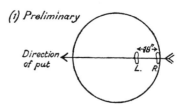

(1) *Preliminary*

Direction of put

The weight is transferred on to the right foot and the left is swung loosely to the rear, as in Pl. XII, 2. It is then kicked powerfully forwards (see Pl. XII, 13), while at the same time the right foot pushes off, lending speed to the movement. The landing is made on the right leg, which should have travelled a third of the way across the ring (see Pl. XII, 3). The left foot moves faster and further than the right, landing a

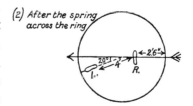

(2) *After the spring across the ring*

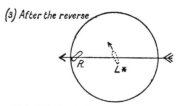

(3) *After the reverse*

* *Left foot will almost certainly be in the air, swinging in the direction of the arrow.*

Fig. 42

fraction of a second later, slightly to the left of it and 6 inches from the toe-board (see Fig. 42, and Pl. XII, 4).

The essence of this movement across the ring is speed. For this reason the right foot should hardly rise from the ground; it executes a sort of "slither", with the spikes only just missing the cinders (for cinders they should be).

(3) *The Put.* Simultaneously on landing the right knee is bent (see Pl. XII, 4, 9, 10) and the upper body is drawn back by a sideways bend from the hips. It is not a twist from the hips, as this would bring the putting arm out of alignment and thereby waste time (see note on 4).

In fact, if anyone were watching the put squarely from the front, the shot should be just visible (and only just so) the whole way across the ring (see Pl. XII, 7–10). In other words, it should not go "round the corner", as it would if the shoulders were twisted backwards.

The power for the "put" is going to be derived from a straightening out of (*a*) the right leg, (*b*) the right side, (*c*) the right arm. These three should flick out simultaneously into a straight line in a perfectly co-ordinated "put" (see Pl. XII, 5 and 11). At this moment (see Pl. XII, 4 and 10) the right arm, which has been maintaining its position as detailed (see Pl. XII, 1), becomes violently active. It drives forwards in exactly the same direction in which it has been moving across the ring and upwards at an angle of 45° (in Pl. XII, 4 it will move along the line of the left arm). The right shoulder will be pushed strongly forwards, aided by a backward and downward sweep of the left arm (see Pl. XII, 4 and 5).

As has been said before, the power behind the shot comes from the straightening out of leg, waist, and arm. To these may be added the forward movement of the right shoulder and the flick of fingers and wrist as the shot leaves the hand.

(4) *The reverse.* A fraction of a second after the shot has left the fingers, the right leg swings forward, the toes hitting the board smartly. The left leg swings backwards and some putters are carried round by the force of their effort till they are facing sideways-on to the direction of their "put". This follow-through movement, called the "reverse", is of the utmost importance, for two reasons. First, it would be impossible to get the weight behind the shot without it, and secondly, it is the only method of not toppling over out of the ring, as it converts the forward momentum into a sideways pivot on the right foot (see rules on p. 151 in Appendix D).

B

9

SOME COMMON FAULTS.

(1) Speed is lost by jumping too high in the air whilst crossing the ring.

(2) Allowing the right hand to get away from the shoulder, instead of bringing it "upwards from under" the shot at the completion of the movement across the ring. This will convert the put into a throwing movement and will make itself felt in the form of a strained elbow.

(3) A badly timed put. Instead of the leg, waist, and arm straightening out together, the arm moves too soon, so that the action of the other two are made of no effect.

(4) Making the put during, instead of before, the reverse. If the shot is sent on its way when both legs are in the air, all drive from the right leg is thereby lost. Here, as in most ball games, steadiness on the feet at the moment of making the "stroke" is essential. In other words, the reverse is important as a follow-through, not as part of the put.

(5) A lack of speed and continuity. The action here has been dealt with on the instalment system, and in practice it may be learnt by taking the parts separately. The finished article, however, should not show anything of this; it should be one smooth, spontaneous whole.

HOW TO LEARN THE "PUT". Shot are made by Messrs Spalding in three sizes, 16 lb., 12 lb., and 8 lb. For those under 16 the 8-pounder will be most suitable, and for the seniors the 12-pounder will be best, though the 16-pounder may be used occasionally in practice. There is no fear of strain for either class if these weights be used; but it is a very sound plan to have a list of those who are going in for shot-putting and allow only the competitors to use the weights. This will prevent boys, who are obviously not strong enough, from hurting themselves by fooling about with the shot.

The footwork. In order to master the technique, the

only sound plan is to practise the footwork separately from the put. This may best be done without the weight. The spring across the ring should be done slowly at first, concentrating on keeping the right foot as near the ground as possible and on landing in the correct position with the waist and leg bent. Care should be taken to see that this position is perfectly poised, as any lack of balance here will considerably lessen the power available for the put. The putting arm also will require careful watching to see that it maintains its position correctly at this stage of the proceedings, the whole tendency being for the elbow to drop into the side and the hand to drift outwards away from the hollow between neck and shoulder, where it should be moored.

This movement across the ring should be practised at first without the shot and then with it, but without completing the put. Remember in tackling this footwork that in the end speed combined with correctness are your aims. One without the other halves the efficacy of the put, and the only way to get both is to start slowly, increasing the quickness of your movements only very gradually. This requires considerable patience, but is infinitely worth it in the long run. The chief danger is that of staleness. Fortunately, however, it is possible to vary the programme of training very considerably, as may be seen from the section on exercises given below.

The Put. Though practised separately, this may be begun at the beginning of the training. The put should be done standing from the position in which the landing is made after the spring across the ring (see Pl. XII, 4). Points to concentrate on are:

(1) Timing the leg, waist, and arm drive so that they act together.

(2) Getting the elbow right behind the shot throughout the action.

(3) To avoid leaning (and looking) away from the line

of the put. In this case the shot will travel a little to the right.

(4) To put at an angle of 45° and follow the shot with your eyes.

(5) The backward and downward sweep of the left arm, which thus assists in bringing the right shoulder forward and upward.

The put should be practised at first without any reverse, as in Pl. XII, 4 and 5. When this has been done successfully, the reverse may be added. This follows on quite naturally, as the whole tendency of the right leg is to follow through in the line of the put, while the left leg also will swing round and behind, as in Pl. XII, 6. The feet should be kept close to the ground, as in the movement across the ring, and the greatest care should be taken to make the reverse a follow-through and not part of the put itself; in other words, the put should not be made during the reverse when the feet are off the ground. A successful follow-through entails the ability to lean after the weight. This movement is made possible by the action of the left leg and arm, as has been explained in the text.

EXERCISES. The following indoor exercises on pp. 39–41 will be found useful for developing those muscles most needed in weight-putting. Nos. 9, 10, 11, for the legs and balance. Nos. 7 and 8 for the stomach. No. 13, especially the sideways bend; keeping the arms outstretched at shoulder height, try to touch the floor first on one side and then on the other. No. 12, for arms and fingers.

Outdoors anything that will produce flexibility and speed is good. The following are recommended: sprinting, starting-practice, high and long jumps with and without a run-up, and for general fitness some quarter-speed striding over distances up to half a mile. For the wrist and fingers, try flicking a shot from one hand to the other.

SOME GENERAL SUGGESTIONS:

(1) Do not bother about distance at first. If you concentrate on style, the distance will come all right.

(2) Practice with a light shot will help to develop speed; but there is much greater temptation to "throw" rather than "put" a light shot, so that probably it is best to work with the one which you will use in competition, though a certain amount of putting with a heavier shot is also useful.

(3) As in all other training, "too little is better than too much". It is a wise plan to limit your work each day to a certain number of efforts; ten "all out" puts is an outside maximum, while six is generally quite sufficient.

(4) Try to get someone to train with you, so that you can watch each other for faults and end up with a few competitive puts.

(5) Do not be disappointed if progress seems slow. It is not an easy business, and "Rome was not built in a day" nor a shot-putter in a week, a month, nor yet a year. Nevertheless there is so much scope for experiment and thought that, if you once begin, it is heavy odds on your becoming as keen about it as those people at Cambridge of whom I have already spoken.

CHAPTER XI

RELAY RACING

THE Greeks in ancient times used to run relay races passing on a lighted torch from one runner to another. Some may regret that this extremely picturesque type of baton is no longer used, and it has at least the merit of giving the poet a fine metaphor for the "team spirit". Relay racing, at any rate, is very far from being obsolete. Ever since the Achilles Club organized the first match between the British Empire and the U.S.A. after the Olympic Games in 1920, this type of racing has become increasingly popular in England.

The reason for this is probably that the relay race has for the spectators an excitement all its own. No one who saw the match at Stamford Bridge between the Empire and the Americans in 1928 will gainsay that. Moreover it does give much more scope for the development of team spirit than the scratch races. This is the chief reason for its spread in the schools throughout the country, and in some places the School Sports are confined entirely to inter-house relays. Personally, although a firm adherent of the relay system, I do feel rather strongly that scratch events, also of course run as an inter-house competition, are very necessary if the possibilities in athletics are ever to be fully developed. This plainly will depend greatly on the amount of time allotted to the Sports, as crowding too much into a short space of time is worse than useless.

In dealing with the technique of relay racing it will be best to split up the subject into strategy and tactics.

STRATEGY. By strategy is meant the arrangement before the race of the order in which the runners shall go. If the figures given here represent the order in which the runners would finish, were they running a scratch race, the two most ordinary schemes are: (a) 4, 3, 2, 1, and (b) 2, 4, 3, 1. In (a) the slowest starts and the fastest finishes, on the principle that the better the man, the more likely will he be to make up lost ground by calling on his reserve speed, of which every runner has more than he thinks. The second order is generally used for races where a good start is of importance. Such are the 4 × 110 yards and 4 × 440 yards, in both of which a lead at the first corner may be a crucial matter; also the Hurdles, where there is a fatal tendency to lose form, hit hurdles, and probably fall when trying to make up distance on a man some yards ahead.

Obviously it is impossible to lay down any hard and fast order of running, as much will depend on the temperament of the runners. Some are much better than others at running by themselves, *i.e.* with a lead, and it may be wise to put such a one to run last, even if he is slightly slower than another who prefers having a man ahead of him. In the jumps and weight-putting it is best to work up to your best man, so that he may know what he has to do.

TACTICS. Tactics include the whole technique of performance on the track.

First and foremost comes the problem of changing over the baton. This should be about a foot long and weigh 2–4 ounces. In the two short relays, 4 × 110 yards and 4 × 220 yards, it should be the aim of the man taking over the baton to be running as fast as the man who is handing over. For effecting the change 20 yards are allowed, 10 on either side of the actual distance. Supposing in Fig. 43 that this is the first change in a race of 4 × 110 yards, *B* would be 110 yards from the start, *A* 100 yards, and *C* 120 yards.

The man taking over will await the incoming runner at *A*. When he reaches a point *X*, the starter will turn his head resolutely to the front and run at full speed with

a perfectly normal sprinting arm action, just as though
there was no one behind him anxious to give him something. Only after 10 yards strenuous acceleration will he
drop his right hand, palm downwards with fingers and
thumb extended. The finisher meanwhile should be just
behind and to the right of the starter. It will be his
business to bang the baton upwards between the fingers
and thumb of the receiver's hand and not let go till the
receiver actually takes it from him. Pl. XIII, A shows the
receiver just grasping the baton and taking it out of the
other's hand. Notice that Jack London, who is receiving,
is looking straight to his front. There should be no
glancing round or checking speed in a well timed change,
by which the baton should be delivered only a yard or
two from C.

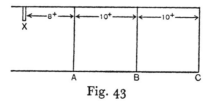

Fig. 43

Immediately on getting the baton into his hand, the
starter should transfer it to his left ready to pass on to the
next man. Some believe in changing into alternate
hands—1 to 2, right into left, 2 to 3, left into right, and
so on. Personally, however, I believe in the left to right
change for each runner who is going to hand on the
baton, especially on a left-inside track. The slight check
to the action caused by the transfer of the baton from
right to left hand by Nos. 2 and 3 seems more than compensated by the fact that it is much easier and more
natural for the receiver to take the baton into his right
hand; moreover he can run on the inside of the track
during the change.

The distance of X from A will depend on the speed of
the finishing runner, which in its turn will depend on

PLATE XIII

A

B

1   2   3   4

C

RELAY RACES

A shows a good change in the sprint relay. In B, 1 should be running straight to his front without looking round—probably he started too soon and had to wait for 4: 2 and 3 are making quite a good change, though it is possible that 2 did not start quite soon enough.

C is a change in a 4 × 880 relay. Note that the receivers are watching the incoming runners, so as to avoid starting too soon.

the distance of the race. The pace at the finish of a 220 yards will be considerably less than that of 110 yards. Another factor is the quickness of the receiver in getting under weigh. This distance therefore must be found by experiment; with first-class sprinters it varies from 12 to 8 yards.

The usual practice in changing over is for the receiver to run with his right hand outstretched till the baton is put into it. The method suggested above was used by the German club which won the 4 × 110 yards relay at the A.A.A. championship this year (1928). Moreover it is not really difficult, as the Achilles team, who were second, also used it with considerable success, though having practised it twice only just before the race. The advantage, of course, lies in the receiver being free to use his arms in the first 10 yards just when he needs them most to generate speed.

This type of change, it must be emphasized, can only be used safely with the two short relays. In a 4 × 440 yards and any distance over, the incoming runner is more than likely to be exhausted and travelling so slowly that any attempt at a running change on the lines suggested above would be fatal (as indeed it was to the English 4 × 400-metre team at Amsterdam). In these longer distances the receiver must watch the incoming runner over his shoulder and time his own start so as to be just on the move at the moment of taking the baton (see Pl. XIII, C). In this case it will also pay to effect the change as near to the back line *A* as possible, so that less distance has to be covered at the fast failing speed of the finisher.

The rule for the backwards-and-forwards race, as in the case of the 4 × 120 Yards Hurdles, speaks for itself and requires no further comment (see p. 11).

Apart from the question of baton-changing, tactics resolve themselves almost entirely into a matter of pace-judgment. Unlike the scratch race, the runner's problem is not merely to beat his opponents, but to win by as many yards as he can. So much has been said about pace-judgment in Chapter v that it seems superfluous to repeat myself here. One matter, however, does seem to need discussion. What is to be done if a runner has a big, but not impossible, deficit to make up? Shall he make his effort and get on terms with the leaders as early as possible in the race, or do so gradually? Unhesitatingly I should advise the second course. Far more effort will be expended in forcing the pace strenuously over the first part of the journey, and, even when the leaders are caught, his bolt will, in all probability, be shot, so that he has nothing left for his finish. The second plan, of slowly cutting down the lead, will be far more economical of effort, though requiring more skill and experience than the other cruder method.

In this matter a personal experience may prove my point. In the final round of the 4×400 metre relay race at the Paris Olympic Games I started on the last stage with an unpleasant deficit to make up on the American. This I did in the first half of the journey, but had nothing left wherewith to press home the advantage gained. My time at the finish was $49\frac{4}{5}$ secs., and as I had run the distance in a shade under 48 secs. in both final and semi-final of the scratch race, I reckon that my lack of judgment in the relay cost me nearly 2 secs., which is about 16 yards; so that, had I run at an even pace throughout, I might well have won instead of being third, as I was. To be really successful as a relay race runner it is in fact essential that a man must know his own optimum pace and have the restraint necessary to hold it at all costs.

APPENDIX A

BIBLIOGRAPHY

GENERAL TEXT-BOOKS ON ATHLETICS

The Athletic Trainer. By H. M. Abrahams. (G. Bell.)
The Complete Athletic Trainer. By S. A. Mussabini. (Methuen.)
Athletics for Boys. By G. R. Renwick. (Herbert Jenkins.)
**Illustrated Text-book of Athletics.* By C. Silverstrand and M. Rasmussen. (Athletic Publications, Ltd.)
**Athletics.* By F. A. M. Webster. (George Allen & Unwin, Ltd.)
**College Athletics.* By Lawson Robertson. (Spalding's Athletic Library.)

BOOKS ON SPECIAL EVENTS

How to Sprint.
Middle Distance and Relay Racing. } Spalding's Athletic Library.
**How to Hurdle.*
**The High Jump.*

* These are especially recommended for the study of field event technique.

AUTO-SUGGESTION

The majority of people who read this book will no doubt consider this section unnecessary and even absurd. Hence its position in the Appendix, so that they need not read it! That auto-suggestion may be of some help to those who suffer from nervousness in an acute form is my hope and belief. From rather bitter experience I know what a curse it may be to live in a state of tension for days, even weeks, before a big event comes off.

Once when I was up at Cambridge, a freshman came along to my rooms on the morning of some College Sports. They were quite a trivial affair, and logically he knew them to be so, but he had hardly slept all the previous night and was moreover quite unable to eat anything. Despite the fact that he was a promising runner with a very good chance of a "Blue", I advised him to give up athletics. I knew that his work would be ruined if he carried on with his running, and at the time there seemed to be no other remedy.

I believe now that such a case can be dealt with by anyone who is determined enough to do so. The determination is necessary, because auto-suggestion is not a very easy habit to acquire, though of priceless value when once a person has it. It would be impossible here to go into the theory of auto- or mental suggestion. At the same time, if anyone is to use it, he must have an idea of how it works.

First let us consider how the nervousness of which I have spoken above attacks one. Generally, with me, it was not a matter of conscious worry; nevertheless it was there, undermining my powers of concentration. Often I have settled down to a morning's work, but despite every effort have been quite unable to take in what I was reading. Always at the back of my mind there was something—a sense of uneasiness which made it well-nigh impossible for my mind to assimilate anything else effectively. At times the "something" would swim up into the surface of my consciousness. When it did, it invariably took the form of a "fear"—"Would I or would I not be running up to form in such and such a race? or should I step out on to the grass at the half distance, as I so often wanted to do?" Such were the doubts and apprehensions lurking below the surface of the mind, causing nervous tension and lack of concentration. At the same time I had difficulty in getting to sleep at night. Here, as a matter of fact, I was helped by a friend who gave me some hints on a sort of auto-suggestion. He told me only half the story, but it nevertheless did get me a lot of sleep which otherwise I should not have got.

Let my own experiences be my excuse for giving here as simply as possible a résumé of the method of auto-suggestion which I believe can be used by anyone, with tremendous gain to himself; certainly it should be of the greatest value to the highly strung person, who will not only sleep better but also save a vast amount of mental and nervous energy so that it may be used, instead of wasted by worrying.

The first thing to do is to let your whole body and mind become completely relaxed. This is not especially easy at first. Generally it is best to think most of the extremities—the toes and ankles, fingers and wrists, for if they are not tensed, the rest of the muscles in the body will follow suit.

Difficulty also may be experienced with the facial muscles, which tend to be particularly obstinate in their refusal to relax. I said also that the mind must be relaxed. Close the eyes, but refrain from shutting them tightly (otherwise you will promptly get facial tension); then concentrate on "sleep". "That", you say, "is all very well, but how on earth am I to concentrate on an abstract idea?" Here the auto-suggestion comes in. You say to yourself, or if you cannot speak aloud, you think the words to yourself: "I'm going to sleep I'm going to sleep very sleepy quite relaxed very happy very drowsy" and so on in other words, with the same idea of calm, peaceful drowsiness as the burden of your murmur. You will notice that I have written the "suggestions" without any punctuation. This is meant, for your voice or thoughts should flow on and on in a continuous sing-song stream with no pause into which other thoughts might enter.

After you have done this for a minute or two—not longer— you should be in a thoroughly relaxed state mentally and physically. Your mind is now in a highly receptive state for any ideas which you may "suggest" to it. If, for example, you affirm that there is *really* nothing to worry about in your athletics (obviously a small thing in the world's history), but on the other hand make quite certain to yourself that you are going to show your best form—and a bit better still, you will have gone a long way to gaining that quiet confidence which is an athlete's greatest asset, because it breeds success.

Now this whole process should not take more than five minutes. It is definitely a mistake to try doing it for a longer period, as if once concentration goes and other ideas creep in when the mind is in this receptive condition, all the good may be undone straight away.

The best times to do it are at night just before going to sleep and directly you wake in the morning. If you can learn to do it in the daytime, it will be invaluable in giving you a new lease of energy. One of the ablest and certainly one of the busiest men I know says that he uses it several times during the day and simply could not carry on unless he did so.

If you are wise, you will not discuss it with your friends. Probably they will be cynically amused, and cynicism does not go happily hand in hand with auto-suggestion. Perhaps you are wondering whether this is "Couéism". It is true that it has points of resemblance, but perhaps the main difference is that in making the suggestions to yourself, instead of being merely mechanical in your repetitions, your mind should be alive to the great things which you will most certainly do.

I have said above that the technique of auto-suggestion is not easy. Do not therefore be surprised or disappointed if you do not get the hang of the thing at once. Make up your mind that you will give it a full trial twice a day for a fortnight at least, and I do not think you will regret it.

PLATE XIV

A

B

C

D

ILLUSTRATING THE USE OF PHOTOGRAPHY IN ATHLETICS

APPENDIX C

THE USE OF PHOTOGRAPHY IN ATHLETICS

Perhaps the greatest difficulty confronting the coach, whether in athletics, cricket, or any other game, is the possession of only one pair of eyes. Suppose for example you are teaching hurdling. If you are wise, you will stand 30 yards away to the side which gives you the best view of the whole action. This will depend on the take-off foot; if it is the right, then you will stand to the right. Well and good—you are now in the right position; but what are you going to look out for? There are plenty of things to choose from—probably about ten in the course of the whole action. The real expert with a trained eye might pick out four with a moderate degree of accuracy, but the ordinary amateur is advised to stick to one at a time.

Much can be done by getting several watchers at different view-points; and this has the additional advantage of stimulating interest. But without doubt the camera, or better still two, one in front and the other either in front or behind, is the ideal method of checking style. Moreover this also stimulates interest to a considerable degree, especially if worked in conjunction with the other method. The best way to do this is to get the watchers to write a short note of criticism on the point of style which they were told to look out for. These might read somewhat as follows: (1) Not enough body-dip in rising to hurdle; (2) too high over hurdle, rear leg not swung through high enough; (3) arms out of control. When the photograph taken of that clearance has been developed, these criticisms can be compared.

Here, however, is met a difficulty. What standard is to be adopted in order that there may be some means of spotting the faults? The answer is that this was one of the main reasons for the lavish illustrations in this book. Let us take an example. Pl. XIV, A and B shows two photos taken of a boy hurdler set side by side with those of Gaby from series B, Pl. VII. By this comparison I was able to see exactly wherein the main fault lay. Contrast the position of the rear leg, and it will at once be obvious that it is being hurried through much too quickly. The whole action therefore shows a lack of balance, which the arm is thrown up to counteract; this will have to be controlled again before it can punch through into the normal running action. Thus straightway I found a fault of form, the righting of which would cause a gain of at least 1 second, probably $1\frac{1}{2}$, on the whole flight.

Plate XIV, C and D gives another series showing the "turn-in-the-air" jump. These would have been more helpful had they been taken from the front, as were those of Simmons, with which they are compared. It is obvious from these photos that the jumper is depending mainly on spring for his height. There is a lack of power in the right (leading) leg as it comes up to the bar, and it would seem to have been lifted rather than swung up, as in the case of Simmons. The style in mid-air is quite good. The absence of a full lie-out is due to the low height at which he is jumping. The last of the series shows that he has completed the turn with a good deal of vigour. Certain faults are, however, apparent. His landing will be made much too far away from the bar, for two reasons: there was too much pace in the run-up, and the rear (right) leg was cut under sideways rather than backwards and downwards. He has bent both legs at the knee, with the result that he will land upon them rather than on his feet.

In long jumping also the camera is useful. Placed exactly opposite to the board, it will show the form at the take-off as nothing else can. In Pl. XV, A is such a photo, and it makes it very plain why an inaccurate run-up detracts from the length of the jump. In this case the jumper is overstriding and reaching out in his effort to hit the board. He has not done this and has lost 8 inches thereby, but he has lost much more by the fact that his body is not over the foot at the moment of driving off, so that he cannot possibly get any "lift" into his jump.

It is indeed difficult to say which event benefits most from the camera-critic. In Putting the Shot it is invaluable. Faults such as allowing the putting hand to get away from the body, putting without both feet on the ground, leaning away from the shot at the moment of putting—all these can be detected by photography with a little experience.

In starting, both the action out of the holes and the body-angle at 25 yards from the start can be examined at leisure when you have photographs taken from the side. Often it is difficult to see with the eye where faults lie in a running action. The camera will show the upright body, the tensed arms, the

PLATE XV

A

B

C

D

ILLUSTRATING THE USE OF PHOTOGRAPHY IN ATHLETICS

Photos C and D are reproduced purely to show that, even with a V.P.K. working at 1/50th sec., it is possible to get results which, *though they cannot hope to be good pictures*, may yet be useful in tracing faults.

kick-up behind—whatever is amiss. Pl. XV, B was taken during the final of a school Mile, when the runners had travelled just under half the distance. All the first three are running in good shape with a nice forward lean, but Nos. 3 and 4 are using too much energy in their arm action for that stage of the race, and No. 4 is also twisting his shoulders instead of keeping them square to the front.

Such are a few of the lessons which may be learnt from the camera. It now behoves me to say something of how action photographs may be best taken. In the first place, unless you have an instrument with a fast lens and shutter, you must not expect to get fine pictures. But, fortunately for the ordinary Brownie or V.P.K. owner, it is not necessary to do this in order to gain a great deal of useful knowledge. Pl. XV, C, for example, was taken of a practise start of my own with an ordinary V.P.K. It is not a good picture, because the definition is poor; but even that may be useful, as it will show which parts of the body are working at speed. Now this was taken too close, about 15–20 ft. away; but if the distance had been double that, although the image would have been smaller, the definition would have been sharper and the body-angle, leg and arm action could have been seen perfectly clearly.

The ordinary camera of the types mentioned above has a shutter speed of 1/50 sec. If you wish to take action photos with this speed of shutter, you must not be too close to the figure. If you wish to take sideway-on snaps, the following table may be a useful basis of experiment, though in the end success is bound to be a matter of finding what your camera will and will not do.

Distance in yards

	Side	45°	Front
Runners sprinting } Long jumpers	35	25	10
Hurdlers, Weight-putters } Middle distance running	25	20	7
High jumpers } Crouch start first stride	20	15	5

A fine day with sunshine is almost a necessity with the ordinary lens and roll-films. It is advisable to mount the camera on a tripod and focus it on the place where the photo is to be taken. You can then concentrate your whole attention on snapping the object at the exact moment. Suppose, for example, you want to take a jumper just over the bar. It will be extremely difficult to do this by looking in the view-finder, which does not give a large enough image for the purpose. Hence the need for a tripod.

In this brief space it is possible to touch only on the fringe of the subject, which has very considerable possibilities of development. An album could be kept with notes on faults and conditions under which the photographs were taken. Lantern slides could be made from some of the good negatives for purposes of lecturing. For the rich the cine-Kodak will give results which of course are beyond the powers of the ordinary camera.

APPENDIX D

EXTRACT FROM RULES
FOR COMPETITIONS

By kind permission of the Amateur Athletic Association

GENERAL RULES

STATIONS

In level races, competitors shall draw for their respective stations at the start.

In straight sprint races, the competitor drawing No. 1 shall take the station on the left facing the winning post, the competitor drawing No. 2 the next station and so on. In races on a circular track, the competitor drawing No. 1 shall take the station nearest the centre of the ground, the competitor drawing No. 2 the next station and so on.

No attendant shall accompany any competitor on the mark or in the race, nor shall any competitor be allowed, without the permission of the Referee or Judges, to receive assistance or refreshment from anyone during the progress of a race.

STARTING

All races shall be started by the report of a pistol, and a start shall only be made to the actual report.

All questions concerning the start shall be in the absolute discretion of the starter, whose decision shall be final. If, in his opinion, the start is not a fair one, he shall recall the competitors.

The Starter shall place competitors on their respective marks in their respective stations, and shall for this purpose have the assistance of such marksmen as he may require.

The starter shall give competitors two warnings:

1. "Get to your marks," then when competitors are ready—
2. "Set," and fire when all competitors are "set," *i.e.,* steady on mark.

If any competitor is unsteady, or for any other reason the starter has to warn a competitor, he shall order all competitors to stand up and then repeat warnings 1 and 2.

No competitor shall touch the ground in front of his mark with any part of his body.

In level races any competitor touching the ground in front of his mark with any part of his body shall be cautioned and for a third offence shall be disqualified.

RELAY RACING

The 400 (4 × 100 yards), and 480 (4 × 120 yards) hurdles relays may be run up and down the track, from standing starts. A warning line will be drawn 1 yard behind the take-over line and each competitor must stand on this, and no part of his body must cross the take-over line until he has been touched on the body (and not the outstretched arm or hand) by the previous runner.

In the event of any competitor in the hurdles race knocking down three hurdles his team is disqualified.

The Mile (4 × 440 yards), 2 miles (4 × 880 yards) and 4 miles (4 × 1 mile) relays will be run round the track, left hand inside. Batons must be carried and exchanged between two lines which will be drawn 10 yards off, and parallel to, the hand-over line. Stations will be drawn for, and lines drawn parallel to the side of the track to denote these stations, and each team will retain its station for handing and taking over throughout the race.

HURDLE RACE

A competitor knocking down three or more hurdles or any part of three or more hurdles, or trailing his leg or foot alongside any hurdle, shall be disqualified.

FIELD EVENTS

GENERAL RULES

Competitors shall take their trials in the order in which their names are printed on the programme, unless the Judges decide to alter that order. A competitor cannot hold over any of his trials to a subsequent round.

TIES:

Should two or more competitors tie, their order shall be decided as follows:—

In jumping for height, three additional jumps shall be allowed at the height at which the competitors failed, and if they still tie, the competition shall be declared a tie.

In those field events where the result is determined by distance, two additional trials shall be allowed and the performances in these trials shall only decide the competition when the competitors exceed the distance at which they tied; otherwise the competition shall be declared a tie.

In the case of a tie, the subsequent performances decide only the relative position of those who are competing to decide the tie.

HIGH JUMP

(a) Any style or kind of uprights or posts may be used. They should be at least 12 feet apart, and shall not be moved during a competition, unless the Judges consider the take off or landing ground has become unsuitable. A change may only be made after a round is completed.

The cross bar shall be entirely of wood and of uniform thickness, and may be circular with square ends, provided it is uniform section throughout, the diameter not to exceed $1\frac{1}{4}$ ins.

Each peg supporting the cross-bar shall be flat and square, $1\frac{1}{2}$ ins. wide and extending $2\frac{3}{8}$ ins. from the upright in the direction of the opposite upright. The end of the cross-bar shall rest on the pegs in such a way that the cross-bar easily falls to the ground, either forward or backwards, if touched by the competitor.

(b) The ground around the take off must be level.

(c) Unless a particular height is specified on the prospectus or entry form, the Judges shall decide the height at which the competition shall start, and the extent to which the bar shall be raised after each round and shall inform the competitors of their decision.

(d) All measurements shall be made perpendicularly from the ground to the upper side of the bar where it is lowest.

(e) Three jumps are allowed at each height, and a competitor failing at the third attempt shall forfeit the right to compete further.

(f) A competitor may commence at any height above the minimum height. He must, however, jump at every following height until, according to (e), he has forfeited his right to compete further.

(*g*) A competitor is entitled to continue jumping at successive heights until he has failed three times at one height, even if all other competitors have failed, and his best jump shall be recorded as the winning height.

(*h*) Neither diving nor somersaulting over the bar shall be permitted.

A fair jump is one where the head of the contestant does not go over the bar before the feet, and is not below the buttocks in clearing the bar.

(*j*) As soon as a competitor makes a spring to jump, this shall be counted as a trial jump.

(*k*) If a competitor passes under the bar without making an attempt to jump it shall not be counted against him as a jump, but three such runs will be counted as one jump.

(*l*) The employment of weights or grips of any kind is forbidden.

(*m*) A competitor may place a mark for his take off and a handkerchief on the cross-bar for sighting purposes.

LONG JUMP

(*a*) A take off board should be fixed in the ground flush thereto. It should be made of wood not less than 4 feet long, 8 inches wide, and 4 inches deep and painted white.

(*b*) The ground in front of the take-off board must not be trenched or dug out, but should be sprinkled with fine sand to a depth of ¼ inch to take an impression and so assist the judges in deciding if a competitor has gone over the take-off line.

(*c*) The length of the run up is unlimited.

(*d*) Each competitor is allowed three jumps; the best three competitors at the end of the first round should be allowed three more jumps. A promoting body may, however, decide a competition by the result of the first round; in such case it must be stated on the programme. Each competitor shall be credited with the best of all his jumps.

(*e*) If any competitor swerves aside at the taking-off line, or the line extended, or touches the ground in front of the take-off board with any part of his foot, such jump shall not be measured, but it shall be counted against the competitor as one jump.

(*f*) The measurement of the jumps shall be made at right

angles from the front (*i.e.*, the edge further from the run up) of the take-off board or scratch line to the nearest break in the ground made by any part of the body of the competitor.

(*g*) The employment of weights or grips of any kind is forbidden.

THROWING AND PUTTING FOR DISTANCE

GENERAL RULES

The circle or scratch line must be clearly marked on the ground by chalk, or otherwise, and all measurements made from the first mark in the ground made by the implement to the inner edge of (*a*) the circle along a line drawn from the mark to the centre of the circle, or (*b*) at right angles to the scratch line, or that line extended. A steel tape should be used for measurement, and that part of the tape showing the feet and inches held by the official at the circle or scratch line.

A foul throw or letting go of the implement in an attempt shall be reckoned as a trial. If an implement break in a fair throw it is not reckoned as a trial.

Each competitor is allowed three trials: the best three competitors at the end of the first round should be allowed three more trials. A promoting body may, however, decide a competition by the result of the first round; in such case it must be stated on the programme. Each competitor shall be credited with the best of all his trials.

In all throwing events from a circle it shall be a foul throw if the competitor, after he has stepped into the circle and started to make the throw, touches with any part of his body or clothing or the implement, the ground outside the circle or if he steps on the circle. The competitor must not leave the circle until the implement has touched the ground, and he shall then from a standing position leave the circle from the rear half, which shall be indicated by a chalk line extended outside the circle.

PUTTING THE WEIGHT

(*a*) The weight shall be put from the shoulder with one hand only, and it must never be brought behind the shoulder.

(*b*) The put shall be made from a circle 7 feet interior diameter.

(*c*) In the middle of the circumference at the front half should be placed a stop-board four feet long, four inches high, and firmly fastened to the ground. In making his puts, the feet of the competitor may rest against but not on top of this board.

The weight shall be of iron or a brass shell filled with lead, and spherical in shape, and shall weigh 16 pounds.

For EU product safety concerns, contact us at Calle de José Abascal, 56–1°,
28003 Madrid, Spain or eugpsr@cambridge.org.

www.ingramcontent.com/pod-product-compliance
Ingram Content Group UK Ltd.
Pitfield, Milton Keynes, MK11 3LW, UK
UKHW030901150625
459647UK00021B/2681